A Practical Guide to Contested Administration Applications for Insolvency Professionals

A Practical Guide to Contested Administration Applications for Insolvency Professionals

Simon Passfield KC
Barrister, Gray's Inn
LLB (Hons) (Nottingham)

Govinder Chambay
Barrister, Inner Temple
LLB (Hons) LLM (Liverpool John Moores University)

Both of Guildhall Chambers, Bristol

Law Brief Publishing

© Simon Passfield KC & Govinder Chambay

All rights reserved. No part of this publication may be reproduced, stored in a retrieval system, or transmitted, in any form or by any means, electronic, mechanical, photocopying, recording or otherwise, without the prior permission of the publisher.

Excerpts from judgments and statutes are Crown copyright. Any Crown Copyright material is reproduced with the permission of the Controller of OPSI and the King's Printer for Scotland. Some quotations may be licensed under the terms of the Open Government Licence (http://www.nationalarchives.gov.uk/doc/open-government-licence/version/3).

Cover image © iStockphoto.com/ljubaphoto

The information in this book was believed to be correct at the time of writing. All content is for information purposes only and is not intended as legal advice. No liability is accepted by either the publisher or author for any errors or omissions (whether negligent or not) that it may contain. Professional advice should always be obtained before applying any information to particular circumstances.

Published 2024 by Law Brief Publishing, an imprint of Law Brief Publishing Ltd
30 The Parks
Minehead
Somerset
TA24 8BT

www.lawbriefpublishing.com

Paperback: 978-1-916698-32-1

PREFACE

In February 2023, we delivered a webinar on contested administration applications as part of Guildhall Chambers' Insolvency Team's Winter Webinar series. Although we were aware that this topic was likely to be of interest to a wide number of insolvency lawyers and practitioners, we were completely unprepared for the extremely high response which the session attracted.

Whilst there are many fine textbooks on insolvency law in general and administrations in particular, there are presently none which focus exclusively on the legal and practical aspects of contested administration applications. We hope that this book will address this.

We have endeavoured to state the law as at 30 January 2024.

Simon Passfield KC & Govinder Chambay
March 2024

CONTENTS

Chapter One	Introduction to Administration	1
Chapter Two	Why Make an Administration Application?	5
	(a) Applications by the company or its directors	5
	(b) Applications by a QFCH	8
	(c) Applications by creditors	8
Chapter Three	Standing to Apply for an Administration Order	11
	(a) Introduction	11
	(b) Categories of persons who have standing to apply	11
	(c) QFCH applications	12
	(d) Standing issues: the company	15
	(e) Standing issues: the directors	19
	(f) Standing issues: the creditors	25
Chapter Four	Jurisdictional Requirements	29
	(a) Introduction	29
	(b) The Test under Paragraph 11(a): the company is or is likely to become unable to pay its debts	29
	(c) Demonstrating cash-flow insolvency: non-payment of specific debt(s)	30
	(d) Demonstrating cash-flow insolvency generally	32
	(e) Demonstrating balance sheet insolvency	34
	(f) Practical Issues	36
	(g) The Test Under Paragraph 11(b): the administration order is reasonably likely to achieve the purpose of administration	36
	(h) The purpose of administration	37

	(i) Disputes as to the application of the Real Prospect Test	39
	(j) Conclusion	45
Chapter Five	The Court's Discretion and Alternative Insolvency Processes	47
	(a) Introduction	47
	(b) Discretion	47
	(c) The views of creditors	48
	(d) The advantages of liquidation	50
	(e) Comparison of outcomes	52
	(f) Making a winding up order	53
	(g) Adjournment	54
	(h) Interim order	54
	(i) Injunctive relief?	55
	(j) Conclusion	57
Chapter Six	Disputes as to the Appropriate Appointees	59
	(a) Introduction	59
	(b) Overarching principles	59
	(c) Disputes between creditors	61
	(d) Disputes between creditors & directors / the company	63
	(e) A middle ground- joint appointment?	69
	(f) Intervention by a QFCH?	71
	(g) Summary of principles	71
	(h) Practical considerations	72
Chapter Seven	Procedure	75
	(a) Administrator's Statement & Consent to Act	75
	(b) The administration application	76

	(c) Supporting witness statement	79
	(d) What should be filed with the court?	81
	(e) Service of the application	81
	(f) How may service be effected?	82
	(g) QFCH intervention?	83
	(h) Application by a QFCH?	84
	(i) Determining the application	84
Chapter Eight	Retrospective Administration Orders	87
	(a) Introduction	87
	(b) Jurisdiction & the test	88
	(c) In context	94
Chapter Nine	Costs	97
	(a) Introduction	97
	(b) Unsuccessful party?	97
	(c) Directors' liability?	102

CHAPTER ONE

INTRODUCTION TO ADMINISTRATION

Prior to the enactment of the Insolvency Act 1986,[1] in most cases the sole insolvency procedure available in respect of an insolvent company was liquidation. This process is something of a blunt tool – since it almost inevitably leads to the cessation of trading – and therefore is unlikely to be appropriate for a company with a potentially viable business capable of being rescued (a point recognised by the Government in 2020, when it introduced temporary measures to restrict the presentation of winding up petitions against companies suffering from temporary liquidity issues as a result of the COVID-19 pandemic[2]). However, in many cases a debenture-holder whose security comprised or included a floating charge over a company's assets and undertaking was given the power to appoint a receiver and manager who could then manage, carry on and/or dispose of the business of the company in order to return it to profitability or maximise the returns to the debenture holder. The Cork Committee recommended that in all cases provision should be made to enable an administrator to be appointed whenever the circumstances justified such a course, with all the powers normally conferred on a receiver and manager appointed under a floating charge, including power to carry on the business and to borrow for that purpose.[3] These recommendations

---

[1] Hereafter, references in this book to sections, unless otherwise stated shall be references to the Insolvency Act 1986.

[2] Corporate Insolvency and Governance Act 2020, Schedule 10.

[3] Cmnd.8558, Ch.9 (paras 495–521).

were carried into effect by the Insolvency Act 1986, which introduced a new administration regime.[4]

Under the original administration regime, an administrator could only be appointed by the court on an application either by the company or the directors, or by a creditor or creditors (including any contingent or prospective creditors) or by all or any of those parties, together or separately[5]. This resulted in a large number of contested applications[6] but relatively few administration orders.[7]

By the Enterprise Act 2002, the original administration regime was replaced with a new regime contained in Schedule B1[8] to the Insolvency Act 1986 with effect from 15 September 2003. Significantly, this conferred on qualifying floating charge holders[9] ("**QFCH**") and the

---

[4] By Part II of the Insolvency Act 1986 (as enacted). Part III of the Insolvency Act 1986 (as enacted) also created a new regime of administrative receivership, but this was subsequently abolished by the Enterprise Act 2002.

[5] Insolvency Act 1986, s.9 (as enacted).

[6] In *Re Rowbotham Baxter Ltd* [1990] BCC 113, various creditors successfully opposed a company's application on the basis that there was no real possibility of the survival of the company and its undertaking as a going concern. In contrast, in *Re Chelmsford City Football Club (1980) Ltd* [1991] BCC 133, various unsecured creditors unsuccessfully opposed a company's application on the basis of an offer to refinance the company. In *Re Far East Abrasives Limited* (HHJ Norris QC, unreported, 1 August 2002), the court granted a creditor's application in the face of opposition from the company. In contrast, in *Re Colt Telecom Group plc* [2002] EWHC 2815 (Ch), the court dismissed a creditor's application where it failed to establish insolvency.

[7] See *Lightman and Moss on The Law of Administrators and Receivers of Companies* (6th ed) at 1-017.

[8] Hereafter, references to paragraphs shall be references to paragraphs within Schedule B1 to the Insolvency Act 1986.

[9] Defined in Insolvency Act 1986, Sch.B1, para.14(2).

company and its directors the power to appoint an administrator out of court in certain prescribed circumstances.

However, creditors other than a QFCH do not have such power and will therefore still need to apply to the court for an administration order in appropriate case. Moreover, there remain a number of circumstances in which it will be necessary or desirable for a QFCH and the company or its directors to make an administration application rather than seek to exercise their power to appoint out of court.

In the following chapters, we will consider the circumstances in which such applications are likely to be made and the bases on which they are likely to result in a contest.

For the sake of completeness this book is concerned with companies in respect of which the courts in England and Wales have jurisdiction to make an administration order – such companies are:

> "(a) a company registered under the Companies Act 2006 in England and Wales or Scotland
>
> (b) a company incorporated in an EEA State or
>
> (c) a company not incorporated in an EEA State but having its centre of main interests in a member State (other than Denmark) or in the United Kingdom."[10]

---

[10] Insolvency Act 1986, Sch.B1, para.111(1A)(a)-(c). The reader should consult specialist works for companies falling outside the scope of the above.

CHAPTER TWO

WHY MAKE AN ADMINISTRATION APPLICATION?

As indicated in the previous chapter, applications for an administration order are less common nowadays because the administration regime in Schedule B1 gives directors, a company and a QFCH the ability to appoint an administrator out of court. Where that route is available, it will ordinarily be more attractive because it is quicker and cheaper.[11]

However, as we consider below, there are a number of circumstances where it may nevertheless be necessary or desirable for the company or its directors or a QFCH to apply formally for an administration order. Moreover, a creditor who does not fit into one of those categories may only obtain an administration order through the courts.

(a) Applications by the company or its directors

Where the directors of a company conclude that a company is insolvent and that an insolvent administration or liquidation is unavoidable, they must treat the interests of the company's creditors as paramount and take every reasonable step to minimise their potential losses. If not, they risk potential claims for breach of fiduciary duty and wrongful trading.[12] In

---

[11] Sealy & Milman: Annotated Guide to the Insolvency Legislation 26th Ed. 2023 (Schedules) Schedule B1 Administration (General Note to Paragraph 10 of Schedule B1 of the Insolvency Act 1986).

[12] *BTI 2014 LLC v Sequana SA & Ors* [2022] UKSC 25 [2022] 3 WLR 709; Insolvency Act 1986, s.214.

the circumstances, they will need to give anxious consideration to the most appropriate insolvency regime and, in particular, whether administration is likely to result in the best return for the company's creditors.

If the directors conclude that administration is more appropriate, they will have ten business days from the filing of a notice of intention to appoint administrators to appoint an administrator out of court.[13] In some cases, there are practical difficulties which prevent an appointment from being made within this period. In such a case, it is possible for the company/directors to file a fresh notice of intention[14] (assuming that the circumstances are not so urgent that there is sufficient time to wait for the period of notice to expire before making the appointment) but they must have a settled and unconditional intention to make the appointment[15] and there is therefore a risk of the fresh notice (and/or any subsequent notices) being challenged as an abuse of process. In the circumstances, the prudent course may be to make an administration application.

Moreover, an administrator cannot be appointed out of court by either a company or its directors when a winding up petition has been presented against the company but has not been disposed of.[16]

Thus, in many cases, seeking an administration order will be a reaction to the presentation of a winding up petition. The interim moratorium under paragraph 44 means that whilst an administration application has

---

[13] Insolvency Act 1986, Sch.B1, para.28(2).

[14] *Re Cornercare Ltd* [2010] EWHC 893 (Ch); [2010] BCC 592.

[15] *JCAM Commercial Real Estate Property XV v Davis Haulage Ltd* [2017] EWCA Civ 267; [2018] 1 WLR 24.

[16] Insolvency Act 1986, Sch.B1, para.25(a). Likewise, if an administration application has been made and has not been disposed of or if an administrative receiver of the company has been appointed. Under these circumstances an administrator may only be appointed via a court order.

been made but has not yet been disposed of the court will not make a winding up order.[17]

The desire by the directors to place the company into administration and avoid a liquidation may boil down to a number of factors; it might be thought that the company is capable of being rescued and therefore that liquidation would be a step too far.

There are other considerations as well – void dispositions[18] do not apply in administration; directors may be concerned to prevent the unravelling of any transactions post-presentation of the petition if it is thought that there are no grounds to obtain a validation order.

Where a winding up petition is extant, it may be that directors turn to a QFCH who, unlike directors or the company, is still capable of exercising their power of appointment under paragraph 14.[19] However, an administration application will be required if in fact the QFCH is unwilling to exercise its power to appoint; they may privately have concerns about the enforceability of their security which commercially they may not wish to reveal (or alert others to by making an application instead of using the out of court process) and they may simply not wish to spend money in making an application if there are others who will do the job of placing the company into administration for them.

There is also the wider question of why administration is preferred over a liquidation. As mentioned, it may be that the company or its directors have identified that there is a real prospect of rescuing the company as a going concern which the making of an administration order would facilitate.

---

[17] Insolvency Act 1986, Sch.B1, paras.42, 43 and 44.

[18] Insolvency Act 1986, s.127.

[19] See Insolvency Act 1986, Sch.B1, para.14 which is not fettered in this respect in the same way as paragraph 22.

(b) Applications by a QFCH

A QFCH may only appoint an administrator out of court of their charge is a 'qualifying' one for the purposes of paragraph 14 and is enforceable. A QFCH who is concerned about whether their charge is enforceable may decide to apply for an administration order instead, because, that way, there is no argument later on about whether the appointment was valid or costly litigation in seeking to rectify the position should it transpire that there were defects in the administrator's appointment.[20]

(c) Applications by creditors

As indicated above, a creditor who is not a QFCH cannot appoint an administrator out of court and must therefore make an administration application.

It is comparatively rare for a threatened administration application to be used as a means of exerting commercial pressure on a debtor company, winding up proceedings being a more obvious tool for this purpose. Rather, the advantage of an administration application is that it is often the most effective means of bringing an insolvent company before the court quickly: given the time periods for advertisement in r.7.10 of the Insolvency (England and Wales) Rules 2016 ("**IR**"), a winding up petition will normally be listed for a first hearing in the general winding up list at least six weeks after it is presented; in contrast, depending on the circumstances, it may be possible to have an administration application heard in the Interim Applications List within a matter of days. This will be particularly advantageous in a case where the creditor has concerns about the way in which the company is being managed by the directors and the risk of increased trading losses or dissipation of assets.

---

[20] *Lightman & Moss on The Law of Administrators and Receivers of Companies* (6th ed) at 6-024.

There are also tactical reasons – a creditor who has in mind a particular appointee may prefer to place the company into administration and have their nominated candidate appointed to obtain a sense of control and direction over the administration. Whilst any such feeling is illusory since administrators are officers of the court[21] and must act independently, to the lay creditor, it is likely to be an important factor.

---

[21] Insolvency Act 1986, Sch.B1, para.5.

CHAPTER THREE

STANDING TO APPLY FOR AN ADMINISTRATION ORDER

(a) Introduction

The effect of not having standing is that the party concerned has no right to apply for an administration order. This should be one of the first things which is checked – an application which is otherwise bound to succeed counts for nothing if a party is not entitled to apply for an administration order. This chapter will explore:

- the categories of persons who have standing to apply;

- applications by a QFCH pursuant to paragraph 35;

- standing issues which can arise in relation to the company and directors;

- the position of creditors with disputed debts.

(b) Categories of persons who have standing to apply

The persons who may apply for an administration order are prescribed by statute.

Paragraph 12 provides that the following may apply:

- the company (paragraph 12(1)(a);

- the directors of the company (paragraph 12(1)(b));

- one or more creditors of the company (which includes contingent and prospective creditors) (paragraph 12 (1)(e) and paragraph 12(4));

- "*The designated officer for a magistrates' court in the exercise of the power conferred by section 87A of the Magistrates' Courts Act 1980*" (paragraph 12(1)(d));

- a combination of persons listed in paragraph 12(1)(a)-(d) (paragraph 12(1)(e)).

Other provisions of the Insolvency Act 1986 give the liquidator of a company[22] and the supervisor of a CVA[23] the ability to apply for an administration order.

Equally, a QFCH may apply for an administration order, as per paragraph 35.

Section 359 of the Financial Services and Markets Act 2000 gives the Financial Conduct Authority standing to apply.

What follows is an analysis of the various standing issues that can and often do arise.

(c) QFCH applications

Paragraph 35 provides as follows:

---

[22] Insolvency Act 1986, Sch.B1, para.38(1).

[23] Insolvency Act 1986, s.7(4)(b) and Sch.B1, para.12(5).

(1) "This paragraph applies where an administration application in respect of a company—

   (a) is made by the holder of a qualifying floating charge in respect of the company's property, and

   (b) includes a statement that the application is made in reliance on this paragraph.

(2) The court may make an administration order—

   (a) whether or not satisfied that the company is or is likely to become unable to pay its debts, but

   (b) only if satisfied that the applicant could appoint an administrator under paragraph 14".

The security must be enforceable; so the conditions necessary to enforce (which will be contained in the security document(s)) must have been triggered.[24] Accordingly, if the security is not enforceable, the charge holder will not have standing to apply under paragraph 35 because the statutory requirements will not be met (although they may be entitled to apply under paragraph 12 as a creditor of the company if they can demonstrate that the company is or is likely to become unable to pay its debts).

The purpose of this procedure is to provide a QFCH with a simple and assured route to realise their security where the company is in default, and to enable any doubts as to the enforceability of the security to be

---

[24] *Sealy & Milman: Annotated Guide to the Insolvency Legislation* 26th Ed-2023 Schedules Schedule B1 Administration (General Note to Paragraph 14 of Schedule B1 to the Insolvency Act 1986).

determined in advance without the administrators being exposed to any risk that an appointment out of court was invalid.[25]

While paragraph 35 does not require a QFCH to demonstrate that the company is or is likely to become unable to pay its debts, they must still show that there is a real prospect of one of the statutory purposes of administration being achieved.[26]

Although the court's power to make an administration order under paragraph 35 is discretionary, where it is satisfied that the QFCH could appoint an administrator under paragraph 14, it should make an administration order unless there are countervailing considerations,[27] such as evidence that the company was solvent or would become so in the near future.[28] There is, so far as the authors are aware, no reported case in which the court has exercised its discretion not to make an administration order under paragraph 35.

A charge remains enforceable even if the company has cross claims against the charge holder.[29]

---

[25] *AIB Group (UK) plc v St. John Spencer Estates & Development Limited* [2012] EWHC 2317 (Ch) at [39].

[26] *Re High Street Rooftop Holdings Ltd* [2020] EWHC 2572 (Ch); [2020] Bus LR 2127 at [13].

[27] *AIB Group (UK) plc v St. John Spencer Estates & Development Limited* [2012] EWHC 2317 (Ch) at [39].

[28] *Hellenic Capital Investments Ltd v Trainfx Ltd* [2015] EWHC 3713 (Ch); [2016] BCC 493 at [25(f)].

[29] *Barclays Bank plc v Choicezone Ltd* [2011] EWHC 1303 (Ch); [2012] BCC 767 at [10].

(d) Standing issues: the company

Paragraph 12(1)(a), on its face at least, empowers a company to apply for an administration order. Since paragraph 12(1)(b) separately provides that the directors of a company may make an administration application, it may be thought that this empowers the members of a company to make such an application. This view is supported by the explanatory notes to the Enterprise Act 2002 which provide:

> *"Appointment by court*
>
> *655. Paragraphs 10-13 set out the court route into administration. A company or its directors, or one or more creditors of a company (which could include a floating charge holder) can apply to court for an administration order (see paragraph 12). The court may only make an order if it is satisfied that the company is, or is likely to become, unable to pay its debts and that the order is reasonably likely to achieve an objective/the purpose of administration (see paragraph 11)."*

The position is far from straightforward, however, as the authorities (less still academics) do not all speak with one voice.

In our view, the members of a company do have sufficient standing to apply if, as a matter of the internal corporate governance of the company, they are able to exercise management of the company's business. The circumstances where that might occur we discuss below.

In *Re Frontsouth (Witham) Ltd*,[30] Henderson J (as he then was) expressed the view, albeit obiter, that where a company's articles of association confer the right of management upon the directors,[31] the members of the company do not have the right to cause the company to apply for an administration order (although by a special resolution they could direct

---

[30] [2011] EWHC 1668 (Ch); [2011] BCC 635 at [31].

[31] As is the case with Article 70 of Table A in the Companies (Tables A to F) Regulations 1985 (as Amended by SI 2007/2541 and SI 2007/2826).

the directors to take such a step). Although, it was ultimately unnecessary for him to decide the point[32] he nevertheless felt it necessary to record his provisional view that:

> *"33......it would be a recipe for corporate chaos, and could be productive of much uncertainty in an area where it is desirable that there should be no room for doubt, if it were open to the shareholders of a company in general meeting to apply to the court for an administration order, or to appoint administrators themselves out of court, at a time when there is a functioning, or potentially functioning, board of directors".[33]*

Similarly, in obiter comments in *Re Assured Logistic Solutions Ltd*[34] HHJ Purle QC observed:

> *"4. As has been pointed out by Henderson J. recently in Re Frontsouth (Witham) Ltd (In Admin.) [2011] EWHC 1668 (Ch); [2011] B.C.C. 635, in the majority of cases adopting standard articles, the only persons who may act for the company are the directors. It is, therefore, somewhat puzzling as to why para.22 makes a distinction between the company and its directors. By way of contrast, in the parallel provisions concerning an application to the court by the directors, the application, once made, is treated as the company's: r.2.3(2) of the Insolvency Rules 1986 (SI 1986/1925),*

---

[32] In *Frontsouth*, the court held that a purported appointment of administrators by the directors out of court was invalid and it was therefore necessary for the court to make a retrospective administration order. It was not practicable for the invalidly appointed administrators to procure the directors to make the application under para.12(1)(b) but after a brief adjournment they were able to persuade the QFCH to do so under para.12(1)(c).

[33] [2011] EWHC 1668 (Ch); [2011] BCC 635 at [33].

[34] [2011] EWHC 3029 (Ch); [2012] BCC 541 at [4-5].

5. There may be cases in which under the constitutional documents of a company there is power in a shareholders' meeting to exercise certain functions of management, including the power to put the company into administration. I cannot myself recall offhand any instance where, in the case of a trading company, I have seen such a division of powers, but it remains a possibility. There is also the power of the company in general meeting to pass a special resolution amending the articles to give the shareholders power to make the appointment."

Conversely, in *Re Eiffel Steel Works Limited*,[35] Andrew Hochhauser QC interpreted the reference to "the company" in paragraph 22(1) as a reference to the members of the company in general meeting. However, this conclusion was not the subject of argument, was obiter,[36] and was apparently made without consideration of Henderson J's comments in *Frontsouth*.

In our view:

- The reference to the company in paragraph 12(1) is a reference to the members of the company in general meeting.

- Parliament cannot have intended to undermine the principle that: (i) the articles must be complied with; and (ii) where the articles bestow the right of management upon the directors (and in the majority of cases the articles will do so) it is not generally

---

[35] [2015] EWHC 511 (Ch); [2015] 2 BCLC 57 at [21].

[36] In *Eiffel*, the court was satisfied that the appointment of administrators pursuant to para.22 was valid notwithstanding the directors' failure to serve notice of intention to appoint on the company and granted the administrators' application for a declaration to this effect. Accordingly, it was unnecessary to consider the company's application for a retrospective validation order.

open to the members to interfere with the directors' decisions,[37] save under certain circumstances.

- Equally, Parliament must obviously have intended that it was open to a company to apply for an administration order.

- Accordingly, in a similar way to the position regarding directors, whether or not a company can apply under paragraph 12(1) falls to be resolved by reference to general principles of company law; essentially, whether as a matter of the internal corporate governance of the company the members can exercise management of the company's business. That represents, in our view, the closest balance between ensuring the provisions of paragraph 12(1) are honoured, whilst also ensuring the orthodoxy of company law is maintained.

As the editors of Reece & Ryan: The Law & Practice of Shareholders' Agreements[38] explain, members can manage the business if the directors do not want to or where they cannot do so. Equally it is open to members all of whom are in complete agreement to amend the articles of the company so as to confer upon themselves the power to exercise management of the company's business.[39] Accordingly, some of the circumstances in which the members will have standing to apply in the name of the company will be:

- where there is no board of directors;[40]

---

[37] *Howard Smith Ltd v And Ampol Petroleum Ltd* [1974] AC 821.

[38] *Reece & Ryan: The Law & Practice of Shareholders' Agreements* (5th ed) at [4.92].

[39] *Cane v Jones* [1980] 1 WLR 1451; [1981] 1 All ER 533.

[40] *Ward (Alexander) & Co Ltd v Samyang Navigation Co Ltd* [1975] 2 All ER 424; [1975] 1 WLR 673.

- where the directors are at an impasse;[41]

- where there is no quorum at a directors meeting;[42] and

- where there is unanimous assent amongst the members that the articles should be amended so as to confer a power on the members to exercise management of the company's business.[43]

It is appreciated that such circumstances will be rare. If they do occur, then the most sensible course of action is to ensure the same is fully evidenced and placed before the court.

(e) Standing issues: the Directors

Cases such as *Minmar (929) Ltd v Khalatschi*[44] and *Re BW Estates Limited*[45] show that a director can only validly appoint an administrator out of court when that decision is by majority and taken in compliance with the company's articles of association. Paragraph 105 cannot be used to rectify the position.

The same principle also applies to in-court applications under paragraph 12, which will mean that the company's constitution will need to be followed.[46] Whilst a more flexible approach was taken to the question of

---

[41] *Barron v Potter* [1914] 1 Ch 895.

[42] *Foster v Foster* [1916] 1 Ch 532.

[43] *Cane v Jones* [1980] 1 WLR 1451; [1981] 1 All ER 533.

[44] [2011] EWHC 1159 (Ch); [2011] BCC 485.

[45] [2017] EWCA Civ 1201; [2017] BCC 406.

[46] *Sealy & Milman: Annotated Guide to the Insolvency Legislation* 26th Ed-2023 Schedules Schedule B1 Administration (General Note to Paragraph 12 of Schedule B1 to the Insolvency Act 1986).

standing in a number of recent cases, that approach, as is explained below, has now been rejected.

Accordingly, if the meeting at which it was decided to apply for an administration order was inquorate for example or was not a decision approved by the majority of the directors, that director will not have standing to apply – the articles of association will not have been complied with.

Re Brickvest Limited[47] was a case which concerned a sole director who applied for an administration order under paragraph 12. There was, however, a serious question as to whether there had been compliance with the articles of association.

The court acknowledged the importance of complying with the company's articles of association when appointing an administrator out of court:

> "*10. The point of difficulty which I must refer to is this. Mr Lumineau is presently the only director of BrickVest Limited, which, as I have said, is the ultimate parent of the group. By Rule 12(1)(b) of Schedule B1 to the Insolvency Act 1986, an application to the court for an administration order in respect of a company may only be made by one of five designated classes of person, one of which is the directors of the company in question. It is clear law that in the case of the appointment of administrators out of court, such an appointment is only regular if the internal rules regarding the company's internal management are properly followed. That, one might think, is self-evidently the case: there must be some form of binary control where the court is not involved in the making of an appointment. Either the resolution appointing the administrator is valid or it is not. If it is valid, then the appointment can take effect. If it is not, then there is an irregularity*

---

[47] [2019] EWHC 3084 (Ch).

that must be cured. The authority that stands for this proposition is Re BW Estate Limited (No.2), [2017] EWCA Civ 1201."[48]

However, the court made no finding of whether the articles had been complied with. As the applications seeking administration orders were made under urgent circumstances, it was considered 'inapt' to consider in detail the company's articles of association or to delay an order that ought to be made whilst an irregular position was being rectified. The court acknowledged that there was a real benefit in making an administration order and that any delay might cause a company to be at risk of trading insolvently which would thwart the purpose of an administration order.

The judge decided that where a serious question arises over a director's standing to make an application for an administration order, the court should treat the matter as a discretionary one, *"taking full account of the question as to standing, but not allowing the point to be automatically determinative against the application"*.[49] It is noteworthy that the court did not consider paragraph 12(1)(b) posed a jurisdictional question of which the court must be satisfied.

In line with the discretionary approach adopted by the court, the court resolved to make an administration order:

"20. Here there is a situation where, through no fault of his own and, more importantly, through no fault of BrickVest Limited, Mr Lumineau is left on his own, the two other directors having recently resigned. In these circumstances, it seems to me that it would be conduct capable of grave injustice were I to refuse to make the orders that are being sought. Accordingly, notwithstanding the issues regarding the BrickVest Limited resolution being by only one director, the jurisdictional requirements in paragraph 11 to Schedule B1 to the

---

[48] ibid. at [10].

[49] ibid. at [19].

Insolvency Act 1986 being met, I should make the administration orders sought."[50]

Re Brickvest is not authority for the proposition that if there has been non-compliance with the articles, the court is nonetheless free to make an administration order. No finding of non-compliance had been made.

Instead, all *Re Brickvest* showed was that where there was a serious question of whether a director has standing (which there must be where there are competing and plausible answers to the question) the court could essentially sidestep that issue and adopt a discretionary approach to the wider question of whether an administration order should be made. Factors relevant to the exercise of the discretion would include whether an administration order would result in a better return for creditors, and the urgency of seeking such an appointment.

Re Brickvest was followed in *Re Nationwide Accident Repair Services Ltd*,[51] a case which concerned a group of 9 companies over which an administration order was sought by the companies' sole director. Nationwide Accident Repair Services Limited ("**NARS**") included amongst the 9 was the non-trading holding company of the group. The articles of association of each of the companies (apart from one) arguably required a quorum of at least two directors before a resolution could be passed. It was possible, therefore, that the director did not have authority to resolve on behalf of those companies to seek the appointment of an administrator. The companies' ultimate parent declined to appoint another director or to amend the articles and indicated that it would not sign a shareholder's resolution to appoint an administrator or consent to NARS' director making such an appointment.

Fancourt J went on to make the administration order. He did not consider that he was prevented from doing so by the absence of any

---

[50] ibid. at [20].

[51] [2020] EWHC 2420 (Ch).

quorum (if more than one was required) and therefore the possibility that the director did not have authority to make the decision.

Following *Brickvest,* and as a matter of principle, there was no impediment, so the court held, to a single director making an application under paragraph 12(1)(b) where they are the sole director, nor would that prevent the court making an administration order where it is otherwise appropriate to do so. The judge held that by virtue of s.6 of the Interpretation Act 1978, the plural form of 'directors' in paragraph 12 would include the singular.

Curiously, the court appeared to have suggested, albeit in *obiter* terms given that there was no finding of non-compliance with the articles, that even if the articles had not been complied with, the directors would have standing to apply:

> "15.…*If the application is made in circumstances in which the board of the company could not resolve to appoint an administrator, that is a matter that the court can take into account in the exercise of its discretion, though it is likely to be outweighed by other relevant considerations in many cases, particularly where, as here, an administration order will result in a better return for creditors and there is no other realistic alternative to a winding up.*
>
> *16. It seems to me that is a case in which a director is the sole appointed director of a company, and that director has standing to apply to the court for an administration order by virtue of para 12(1)(b) of Schedule B1, even if under the internal governance of the company he could not alone pass a resolution of the company to make such an application. The Court will then exercise its discretion, taking into account all relevant circumstances, which may include the reasons why there is a sole director and the effect of the company's articles as to the relevant powers of its board."*[52]

---

[52] [2020] EWHC 2420 (Ch) at [15]-[16].

Re Brickvest and *Nationwide* are both cases which show pragmatism over principle. The issue of non-compliance was essentially side-stepped in *Brickvest* in favour of looking at the bigger picture and not allowing a potential defect to stand in the way of an administration order which, on the facts, needed to be made.

The discretionary, pragmatism-over-principle approach was brought to an end in *Re Lyhfl Limited*,[53] in which the court departed from *Brickvest* and *Nationwide* and concluded that a director does not have standing to make an administration application when there was neither a decision by the majority of the board nor a valid resolution of the board in favour of the application.

In *Re Lyhfl*, the court departed from *Brickvest* on the basis that (i) paragraph 12, read with para 105, means that a majority of the board is required; (ii) the same approach which is adopted in respect of out of court appointments should also apply to paragraph 12 given that the language in paragraph 12 is identical to paragraph 22(2); (iii) whilst *Minmar, BW Estates and Re Equiticorp*[54] were not decisions on paragraph 12, they provide clear support for the meaning of paragraph 12 and did not appear to have been sufficiently drawn to the court's attention in *Brickvest*; (iv) the court cannot of its own motion appoint an administrator; it may only do so by an application by one of the permitted categories of persons; and (v) r.12.64 IR cannot dispense in advance with jurisdictional requirements.[55]

Nationwide was distinguished on the footing that that case concerned a sole director.[56]

---

[53] [2023] EWHC 2585 (Ch).
[54] [1989] 1 WLR 1010; (1989) 5 BCC 599.
[55] [2023] EWHC 2585 (Ch) at [19]-[23].
[56] ibid. at [22].

Accordingly, the position as a matter of law is contained in *Re Lyhfl* which expressly departs from *Re Brickvest* and impliedly departs from *Nationwide* insofar as the latter suggests that a director has standing to apply even where the articles have not been complied with.

Re Lyhfl represents the current and correct position regarding paragraph 12. That being said, one can see the instinctive appeal of adopting the pragmatism-over-principle approach taken in *Re Brickvest* where it is clear that an administration order needs to be made and where it is likely to be of benefit.

However, as matters stand currently, the law is clear – a director will not have standing to apply for an administration order if the decision is not one of the majority and fails to comply with the company's internal rules of governance.

(f) Standing issues: creditors

Contingent and prospective creditors have standing to apply for an administration order. Thus, in *Re British American Racing (Holdings) Ltd*[57] an administration order was made on the application of a substantial creditor of the company for future debts becoming due on the maturing of loan stock.

A party has standing to apply for an administration order as a creditor even where their debt is disputed on substantial grounds if they can show that they have a good arguable case that a debt of sufficient amount is (or, in the case of a contingent or prospective creditor, may or will become) owing to them. It is then a matter for the discretion of the court whether actually to make an administration order. The court has jurisdiction to deal with the application without having to resolve the

---

[57] [2004] EWHC 2947 (Ch); [2005] BCC 110.

dispute about the debt.[58] The same position applies where the company claims to have a genuine and substantial cross-claim against the applicant which equals or exceeds the applicant's debt.

However, attaining creditor status for the purpose of having standing to present the application does not mean that the applicant is a creditor "*for the purposes of section 123(1)(a) or that the amount of his alleged debt is a debt or liability for the purposes of section 123(1)(e) or (2)*".[59] Thus, the same evidence which is sufficient for the purposes of locus standi is not necessarily sufficient to persuade a court that a company is unable to pay its debts (and thus that the conditions for making an administration order are met) or that it should exercise its discretion to make an administration order. We will consider these issues further in the next chapter.

But where the court is satisfied that it would be appropriate to make an administration order, it is unlikely to decline to do so on the basis that there is a substantial dispute in relation to the applicant's debt. This is in marked contrast to the position in relation to winding up petitions[60] and reflects the significant differences between the two insolvency regimes.

---

[58] *Hammonds (a firm) v Pro-fit USA Ltd* [2007] EWHC 1998 (Ch); [2008] 2 BCLC 159 at [53].

[59] ibid. at [54].

[60] In *Mann v Goldstein* [1968] 1 WLR 1091 at 1098f, Ungoed-Thomas J held that a creditor whose debt is disputed on substantial grounds does not have standing to present a winding up petition. That analysis was adopted by the Court of Appeal in *Stonegate Securities Ltd v Gregory* [1986] Ch 576 at 579G. However, as Warren J noted in *Hammonds (a firm) v Pro-fit USA Ltd* [2007] EWHC 1998 (Ch); [2008] 2 BCLC 159, this was inconsistent with the earlier decision of the Court of Appeal in *Re Claybridge Shipping Co SA* [1997] 1 BCLC 572, in which Lord Denning MR indicated that the court had jurisdiction to hear a disputed debt petition but would only do so in exceptional circumstances. In *Khan v Singh-Sall* [2023] EWCA Civ 1119, Nugee LJ indicated that the approach

in *Claybridge* is the correct one: i.e. a creditor with a disputed debt has standing to present a winding up petition but since the court will not as a matter of practice decide if there is in fact a debt, they will not in practice be able to obtain a winding up order.

CHAPTER FOUR

JURISDICTIONAL REQUIREMENTS

(a) Introduction

With the issue of standing surpassed, an applicant for an administration order under paragraph 12 must satisfy the two jurisdictional requirements contained in paragraph 11 before the court has a discretion to make an administration order. Those requirements are:

(a) "that the company is or is likely to become unable to pay its debts, and

(b) that the administration order is reasonably likely to achieve the purpose of administration."

These requirements are cumulative and both must be satisfied. If they are not, the applicant can progress the application no further.

This chapter will focus on those jurisdictional requirements.

(b) The Test under Paragraph 11(a): the company is or is likely to become unable to pay its debts

The first hurdle for the applicant to overcome is to demonstrate that it is more probable than not that the company is or will become unable to pay its debts.[61] In this regard, the phrase "unable to pay its debts" has the

---

[61] *Re AA Mutual International Insurance Co Ltd* [2004] EWHC 2430 (Ch) at [21].

same meaning as in s.123 IA (which relates to winding up petitions).[62] Therefore, the usual 'cash-flow' insolvency or 'balance sheet' insolvency tests will apply. We will now consider these in turn.

(c) Demonstrating cash-flow insolvency: non-payment of specific debt(s)

Section 123(1)(e) provides that a company is "deemed" unable to pay its debts if "it is proved to the satisfaction of the court that the company is unable to pay its debts as they fall due".

As Lord Walker explained in *BNY Corporate Trustee Services Ltd v Eurosail–UK 2007–3BL plc*[63] this is not a true deeming provision:

> "25....It does not treat proof of a single specific default by a company as conclusive of the general issue of its inability to pay its debts... It may open up for inquiry a much wider range of factual matters, on which there may be conflicting evidence. The range is wider because section 123(1)(e) focuses not on a single debt (which under paragraphs (a) to (d) has necessarily accrued due) but on all the company's debts "as they fall due" (words which look to the future as well as to the present)".[64]

Ultimately, the question for the court is whether the company is able to pay both its presently due debts and debts falling due from time to time in the reasonably near future.[65]

At first blush, it may be thought that this will require the court to undertake a careful analysis of the company's full trading history in order to ascertain the true cashflow position. However, it is nevertheless

---

[62] Insolvency Act 1986, Sch.B1, para.111(1).
[63] [2013] UKSC 28; [2013] 1 WLR 1408.
[64] ibid. at [25].
[65] ibid. at [37].

commonplace (indeed, customary) for a winding up petition successfully brought on the ground in s.123(1)(e) to rely solely on the debtor's failure to pay a single specific debt to the petitioner. In *Doran v County Rentals Limited (t/a Hunters)*,[66] the court summarised the relevant principles in this regard as follows:

- Where a debt is due and an invoice has been sent and the debt is not disputed, the failure to pay the debt is itself evidence of an inability to pay unless there is a substantial reason for non-payment. A bad reason put forward honestly is insufficient, however.[67]

- Although s.123(1)(e) enables the court to come to the conclusion that a company is unable to pay its debts as they fall due on any evidence which satisfies it of that fact and it is not necessary that there be a demand at all, the court should be slow to reach such a conclusion from the mere non-payment of a debt which has never been demanded of the company.[68]

- The company should have had an opportunity to pay the undisputed debt.[69]

- Section 123(1)(e) requires the court to determine whether the ground is made out at the time of the hearing of the winding up.[70]

---

[66] [2022] EWCA Civ 1376; [2023] BPIR at [14].

[67] *Cornhill Insurance plc v Improvement Services Ltd* [1986] 1 WLR 114; (1986) 2 BCC 98942 and *Re Taylor's Industrial Flooring Ltd* [1990] BCC 44 per Dillon LJ at 50B -D.

[68] *Re A Company (No.006798 of 1995)* [1996] 1 WLR 491 per Chadwick J at 502D.

[69] *Re Easy Letting & Leasing* [2008] EWHC 3175 (Ch) per Morgan J at [11].

[70] *Re A Company* [2022] EWHC 1690 (Ch) per Miles J at [54].

It follows that a creditor who applies for an administration order should be able to satisfy this jurisdictional requirement simply by demonstrating that it is owed an undisputed debt which the company has not paid. However, as noted above, where the creditor's debt is disputed by the company, the creditor is likely to need to go further and either prove their claim on the balance of probabilities[71] or identify alternative grounds for concluding that the company is cashflow insolvent.[72]

(d) Demonstrating cash-flow insolvency generally

Where a company or its directors apply for an administration order on the footing that the company is cashflow insolvent, they will normally be expected to provide disclosure of the company's relevant accounting records (including the latest internal financial reports and cashflow projections) to evidence this.[73] This will then enable any interested party (such as an investor or minority shareholder) who wishes to challenge the position or explore a solvent rescue of the company to do so.

Similarly, a creditor who is unable to demonstrate insolvency by reference to a specific undisputed and unpaid debt owed to them may nevertheless seek to satisfy the court that the company is cashflow insolvent by reference to its trading position as a whole (although this may prove difficult in practice without access to the relevant extensive accounting information).

---

[71] *Re Berkshire Homes (Northern) Ltd* [2018] EWHC 938 (Ch); [2018] Bus LR 1744 per HHJ Hodge QC at [38].

[72] See *Fieldfisher LLP v Pennyfeathers Ltd* [2016] EWHC 566 (Ch); [2016] BCC 697, in which the court could not be satisfied that the company was unable to pay its debts where the applicant relied solely on a disputed debt that was subject to an arbitration clause.

[73] *Insolvency Litigation: A Practical Guide* (3rd ed) at 6-019.

The principles underlying the cash flow test demonstrate that its application is not an exact science. Some of those principles, along with some practical guidance is given below:

- Contingent and prospective liabilities in the near future can be taken into account.[74]

- Precisely how far into the future one may look depends on all the circumstances and the nature of the company's business; once the court moves beyond the reasonably near future, the cash flow test becomes speculative.[75]

- The court may consider what a company can obtain by realising assets within a relatively short time – the key here will be establishing the likelihood (or the opposite) of such assets being sold in a short time.[76]

- A company that is able to pay its debts by borrowing money is *prima facie* able to pay its debts.[77] However, the Court of Appeal have indicated that such a company may be treated as 'commercially' insolvent on cash flow or a balance sheet basis.[78] Consider therefore how the company is meeting its liabilities.

---

[74] *Re Cheyne Finance plc* [2007] EWHC 2402; [2008] 2 All ER 987 at [53]; *BNY Corporate Trustee Services Ltd and others v Eurosail-UK 2007–3BL plc* [2013] UKSC 28; [2013] 1 WLR 1408 at [37].

[75] [2013] UKSC 28; [2013] 1 WLR 1408 at [37].

[76] *Re Capital Annuities Ltd* [1979] 1 WLR 170; [1978] 3 All ER 704 at 182F-G.

[77] *Re A Company* [1986] BCLC 261 at 262E.

[78] *Bucci v Carman* [2014] EWCA Civ 383; [2014] BPIR 523 at [31].

- In *Re Hat & Mitre plc (In Administration)*[79] Trower J said: "*I agree that neither an insufficiency of cash to pay immediate liabilities nor a need to borrow to pay short term liabilities are necessarily an indication of a present inability to pay debts; all the circumstances of the case must be looked at*". The first half of that proposition must refer to circumstances where a company is suffering a very temporary liquidity crisis or will have a sufficient injection of funding in short order.

- Cash flow insolvency has been found in cases where there are: (i) unpaid judgments;[80] (ii) admissions of an inability to pay[81] and (iii) no/insufficient assets to enforce against.[82]

(e) Demonstrating balance sheet insolvency

By s.123(2), a company is also "deemed" unable to pay its debts if "it is proved to the satisfaction of the court that the value of the company's assets is less than the amount of its liabilities, taking into account its contingent and prospective liabilities". Again, this is not a true deeming provision.

Some general principles are as follows:

- The starting point is that if a company's immediate liabilities exceed its assets, the Company is unable to pay its debts. There is then an

---

[79] [2020] EWHC 2649 (Ch) at [106].
[80] *Re Tweeds Garages Ltd* [1962] Ch 406; [1962] 2 WLR 38.
[81] *Re Great Northern Copper Co* (1869) 20 LT 264.
[82] *Re Douglas Griggs Engineering Ltd* [1963] Ch 19; [1962] 2 WLR 893 at [23].

evidential burden on the company to establish why, notwithstanding its balance sheet, it can reasonably be expected to meet its liabilities.[83]

- Contingent and prospective liabilities can be taken into account, but not contingent and prospective assets – so assets which may in the future become the company's or which are contingent on the company's subsequent insolvency do not form part of the assessment.[84]

- Establishing balance sheet insolvency is not a simple comparison of the company's assets and liabilities as recorded in the accounts. The court must consider whether the company's asset position means that it will be unable to meet its liabilities.[85]

- The more distant a liability is, the more difficult it is to establish it.[86]

- The ability of a company to meet its prospective and contingent liabilities is to be determined on the balance of probabilities with the burden of proof on the party asserting balance-sheet insolvency.[87]

- In respect of the burden of proof, in *Synergy Agri Holdings Ltd v Agform Ltd*[88] the approach the court followed was that the petitioning creditor was required to prove that the company was unable to pay its debts, following which the company became subject to an

---

[83] *Re Casa Estates (UK) Ltd* [2013] EWHC 2371 (Ch) at [81].

[84] *Evans v Jones* [2016] EWCA Civ 660; [2016] BPIR 1207 at [19]-[20].

[85] *BNY Corporate Trustee Services Ltd v Eurosail-UK 2007-3BL Plc* [2011] EWCA Civ 227 at [42]-[49].

[86] ibid. at [119].

[87] [2013] UKSC 28; [2013] 1 WLR 1408 at [34].

[88] [2020] EWHC 343 (Ch).

evidential burden to rebut insolvency (albeit the same was described as a low hurdle).

(f) Practical Issues

First, as commentators have observed, a court will likely be persuaded by a director who says that a company is unable to pay its debts because they will very likely have the evidence available to them to support such a contention.[89]

Conversely, creditors will not have the same amount of knowledge as directors about the company's dealings and should therefore try to obtain as much knowledge as they can from sources which can be viewed by anybody along with knowledge which it has obtained through its own dealings with the company in order to provide as much as it can about the company's affairs.[90]

For a case in which the court was not satisfied of matters under Paragraph 11(a) see *Green v Gigi Brooks Ltd*.[91]

(g) The Test Under Paragraph 11(b): the administration order is reasonably likely to achieve the purpose of administration

Having established insolvency to the requisite standard of proof, the applicant must then demonstrate that there is a "real prospect" that the administration order will achieve the purpose of administration.[92] This is a lower test than the balance of probabilities test; the applicant is

---

[89] *Lightman & Moss on The Law of Administrators and Receivers of Companies* (6th ed) at 6-028 – 6-032.

[90] ibid.

[91] [2015] EWHC 961 (Ch).

[92] [2004] EWHC 2430 (Ch); [2005] 2 BCLC 8.

required to show a "realistic" as opposed to a "fanciful" prospect that the purpose of administration will be achieved.[93]

(h) The purpose of administration

The statutory purpose of an administration is to be found in paragraph 3(1) which provides that:

> "The administrator of a company must perform his functions with the objective of—
>
> (a) rescuing the company as a going concern, or
>
> (b) achieving a better result for the company's creditors as a whole than would be likely if the company were wound up (without first being in administration), or
>
> (c) realising property in order to make a distribution to one or more secured or preferential creditors."

These objectives are hierarchical.[94]

It is not necessary for an applicant to identify in advance with certainty which of the statutory objectives will be obtained,[95] although in practice one will invariably have to discuss one or more in isolation.

In practice, it is very rare for an administrator to pursue objective (a), as the circumstances in which it will be possible to rescue the company (as

---

[93] *Swain v Hillman* [2001] 1 All ER 91.
[94] Insolvency Act 1986, Sch.B1, para.3(3) and (4).
[95] *Hammonds v Pro-Fit USA* [2007] EWHC 1998 (Ch); [2007] 2 BCLC 159.

opposed to its business) as a going concern are necessarily very limited. For a rare example of such a case, see *Re Gate Ventures plc*.[96]

Accordingly, in most cases the applicant will focus on objective (b) and seek to demonstrate that administration is likely to be a better alternative for the company's creditors than liquidation. This should be relatively easy to establish where it is envisaged that the administrators will be able to preserve the company's business and assets as a going concern or that a continued period of trading will enable a more orderly winding up of the company's affairs than could be achieved in liquidation. However, where this is not the case, there may be little practical difference between an administration and a liquidation. Prior to 2016, it was common in such cases for applicants to argue that administration was necessarily the better option because the liquidation was inevitably a more expensive process as a result of the liquidator's statutory obligation to pay *ad valorem* fees. However, these have since been abolished[97] and therefore this argument is now unlikely to carry any real weight in many cases.[98]

In cases where the applicant cannot show a real prospect of a better result for unsecured creditors in administration than liquidation, they may seek to fall back on objective (c) and focus on achieving a return to the secured creditor(s). However, an administrator can only pursue this objective if they do not unnecessarily harm the interests of the company's creditors as a whole.[99] In *Re Baltic House Developments Ltd*,[100] the court was not satisfied that this would be the case where the evidence demonstrated that administration was likely to be more costly than liquidation and there

---

[96] [2020] EWHC 709 (Ch).

[97] Insolvency Proceedings (Fees) Order 2016/692.

[98] For a recent example of where this argument was accepted (albeit on unusual facts) see *Coote v Astrosoccer 4 U Ltd* (Lesley Anderson QC, unreported, 7 December 2017).

[99] Insolvency Act 1986, Sch.B1, para.3(4).

[100] [2018] EWHC 1525 (Ch); [2018] Bus LR 1531.

was no identifiable benefit in proceeding with administration that made that additional cost worthwhile.

(i) Disputes as to the application of the Real Prospect Test

As indicated above, disputes as to whether the condition in paragraph 11(b) is satisfied are most likely to arise where the applicant contends that there is a real prospect of objective (b) being achieved (i.e. that an administration will achieve a better result for unsecured creditors than an immediate liquidation).

The proper approach to the test in this context was helpfully summarised by Warren J in *Auto Management Services Ltd v Oracle Fleet UK Ltd*:

> "3. There is no dispute about the applicable principles. There has to be a real prospect that the administration order will achieve the purpose. That does not mean that I need to be satisfied that on the balance of probabilities there will be a better outcome upon administration as compared with winding up. There has to be a real prospect. It is not enough to show a real prospect that administration would achieve no worse an outcome. The prospect of a better result must be shown. However, I venture to think that if an administration can be shown in all but the most unlikely circumstances to produce a result no worse than liquidation, and if it can be shown that there are reasonably possible circumstances in which administration can in fact produce a better result so that paragraph 11(b) is satisfied, that will be a significant factor when it comes to exercising a discretion whether or not to make an order."[101]

It is clear from this that the burden of demonstrating a real prospect of objective (b) being achieved is not a particularly onerous one. It is nevertheless important for the applicant to ensure that they have adduced

---

[101] [2007] EWHC 392 (Ch); [2008] BCC 761 at [3].

sufficient evidence to meet the (admittedly low) test. In this regard, the following principles can be derived from the leading cases:

- The evidence put forward should be cogent and compelling (albeit keeping in mind the underlying context of demonstrating a real prospect).[102]

- The evidence should also be reliable, in the sense that (1) a clear account is given of all potentially relevant facts and circumstances, and (2) where explanators are given or judgments, estimates or opinions are stated (a) they should be supported by the underlying material, and not contradicted by it, and (b) they should also be credible in the sense of being realistically likely to be true.[103] However, what is required to meet this standard depends on the circumstances. The expectations of the product of a director (assuming them to have been in office for a sufficient period) are likely to be very different to the product of a creditor. Further, so far as the relevant opinion and views regarding administration are likely to be those of the proposed administrators, what is expected of them, in circumstances where they have had no prior dealings the company is also bound to be different.[104]

- It should give some thought and detail on how the practical mechanics of a given purpose might be achieved; for instance: details of any funding which might be available in the case of selling property and details of any support which a lender might

---

[102] [2018] EWHC 1525 (Ch); [2018] Bus LR 1531.

[103] *Re Bowen Travel Limited* [2012] EWHC 3405 (Ch); [2013] BCC 182 at [19].

[104] *Hartley Pensions Limited v Wilton UK (Group) Limited* [2023] EWHC 1700 (Ch) at [106].

- be prepared to give to assist with rescuing a company as a going concern.[105]

- The evidence should explain what the administrators are proposing to do in the immediate future and with what result or how this would compare if no order was made.[106]

- In order properly to address the matters set out above, it is generally sensible for the proposed administrators to provide a witness statement or report to amplify the matters set out in the applicant's own evidence. The proposed administrators must do so carefully, with an independent mind, and on the basis of a critical assessment of the position of the company and the proposals put forward.[107]

Where the applicant is relying on objective (c), any dispute is likely to focus on whether that objective can be achieved without causing unnecessary harm to the creditors.

Examples of cases where an applicant has satisfied the court that there was a real prospect of the purpose of administration being achieved in the face of opposition include:

- *Re Redman Construction Limited*[108] – a company applied for an administration order and relied on a witness statement from its director to the effect that the company had a number of profitable contracts to complete and a report from the proposed administrator that on that basis, the deficiency to creditors would be less in administration than liquidation. An opposing creditor pointed out a number of shortcomings in the evidence but the

---

[105] [2018] EWHC 1525 (Ch); [2018] Bus LR 1531 at [37-38].
[106] *Green v Gigi Brooks Ltd* [2015] EWHC 961 (Ch) at [31].
[107] *Re Integral Ltd* [2013] EWHC 164 (Ch) at [69].
[108] [2004] EWHC 3468 (Ch).

court was nevertheless satisfied that it was sufficient to conclude that there was a real prospect of the purpose being achieved.

- *Coote v Astrosoccer 4 U Ltd*[109] – the evidence demonstrated a realistic prospect of a sale of the company's business and assets (which could not be achieved in liquidation) and the costs of administration were significantly lower than liquidation.

- *DKLL Solicitors v HMRC*[110] – two equity partners in a firm of solicitors which was a limited liability partnership applied for an administration order in relation to the partnership in order to enable a pre-pack sale of its business and assets to be effected. In support of their assertion that there was a real prospect of objective (b) being achieved, the partners relied on an estimated statement of affairs prepared by the proposed administrators which showed that realisations in liquidation would be substantially lower than in administration. HMRC (a substantial creditor) challenged this. Andrew Simmonds QC held that the court could place great reliance on the expertise and impartiality of the proposed administrators and noted that HMRC had produced no evidence to support its assertion that the estimated statement of affairs was inaccurate.

- *Re Professional Computer Group Limited*[111] – a company applied for an administration order in order to preserve its business as a going concern pending a sale, thereby enabling objective (b) to be met. A major creditor argued that there was no real prospect of this happening because it would block the administrator's proposals. Morgan J rejected that argument on the basis that it was not established that the creditor was the majority creditor

---

[109] Lesley Anderson QC, unreported, 7 December 2017.
[110] [2007] EWHC 2067 (Ch); [2007] BCC 908.
[111] [2008] EWHC 1761 (Ch).

and it would in any event be open to the administrator to seek approval of the court to their proposals, which the court might give if the proposals were judged to be in the interests of creditors generally.

Examples of cases in which the applicant failed to satisfy the court that there was a real prospect of the purpose of administration being achieved include:

- *Re Ci3net.com Inc*[112] – a bank applied for an administration order in respect of a holding company incorporated in the USA. There was no prospect of that company being rescued as a going concern, no evidence that more might be received for the companies' assets in administration than liquidation and no secured or preferential creditors to whom a distribution could be made.

- *Re AMCD (Property Holdings) Limited*[113] – in response to a winding up petition, the director of a company applied for an administration order. The only purpose of administration identified in the evidence was to recover a book debt. There was no better prospect of recovering that debt in administration rather than liquidation.

- *Re Bowen Travel Limited*[114] – the applicant director's evidence was contradicted by underlying documents in material respects, important matters were not addressed in that evidence, the company's bankers had refused to extend the company's bank facilities, the termination of a major contract caused a foreseeable and material decline in the company's business and the company's solvency had for years been propped up by the

---

[112] [2004] EWHC 1941 (Ch); [2005] BCC 277.
[113] [2004] EWHC 3463.
[114] [2012] EWHC 3405 (Ch); [2013] BCC 18.

- *Data Power Systems Ltd v Safehosts (London) Ltd*[115] – there was no sufficiently cogent credible evidence that a company which had not traded or established itself as a going concern was capable of becoming a going concern and there was no evidence that the creditors were likely to benefit either from a rescue or from any dividend in the event that the company was placed into administration.

- *Green v Gigi Brooks Ltd*[116] – the applicant's evidence was so thin that it was not sufficient to enable the court to be satisfied that the purposes of administration would be reasonably likely to be fulfilled.

- *Re Baltic House Developments Ltd*[117] – a company which owned an incomplete development applied for an administration order. This was opposed by a number of unsecured creditors. The company initially proposed that the administrators should sell the development in its incomplete state. The company relied on an estimated outcome statement prepared by the original proposed administrator which showed a modestly better recovery in administration than liquidation (23.3p in £ v 20.3p in £). This was subsequently revised to show a more marginal potential benefit in administration (14.5p in £ v 13.2p in £) and this was based solely on the costs of liquidation being significantly greater. As a result, the original proposed administrator was no longer prepared to act. The company therefore sought the appointment of alternative proposed administrators on the basis that objective

---

[115] [2013] EWHC 2479 (Ch); [2013] BCC 721.
[116] [2015] EWHC 961 (Ch).
[117] [2018] EWHC 1525 (Ch); [2018] Bus LR 1531.

(c) could be met. At the eleventh hour, the alternative proposed administrators prepared a report in which they suggested that objective (b) could be met by either completing the development or selling it to a party prepared to give enhanced funding because of the potential completion. HHJ Eyre QC (as he then was) held that the material put forward was neither cogent nor compelling and was on proper analysis very limited. Accordingly, he was not satisfied that there was a real prospect that objective (b) could be met. Moreover, in light of the evidence from the unsecured creditors that liquidation would be cheaper than administration, he held that there was no real prospect that objective (c) could be met without unnecessarily harming the interests of the company's creditors as a whole.

(j) Conclusion

In summary:

- The test under paragraph 11(a) is whether it is more probable than not, whereas under paragraph 11(b) the test is whether there is a real prospect.

- Although cash-flow insolvency is not an exact science, generally speaking an inability to meet current demands or demands in the very near future will strongly point towards cash flow insolvency unless there is evidence which shows the Company is suffering a very temporary liquidity crisis or will have an injection of funding in short order.

- Balance sheet insolvency is not simply a question of whether liabilities exceed assets; the court must consider whether the company's asset position is of such that it will be unable to meet its liabilities.

- The burden of proof in showing balance sheet insolvency lies on the party who alleges the company is insolvent which then results in an evidential burden being imposed on the company to rebut balance sheet insolvency.

- Demonstrating a real prospect involves, *inter alia*, adducing evidence which is cogent and compelling, and gives real thought to the practical mechanics of how a given purpose might be achieved.

CHAPTER FIVE

THE COURT'S DISCRETION AND ALTERNATIVE INSOLVENCY PROCESSES

(a) Introduction

Let us assume that issues of standing have been surpassed, and the court is satisfied that it has jurisdiction to make an order under paragraph 11. The question then is whether the court should exercise the discretion which it has to make an administration order under paragraph 13.

That discretion can be exercised in ways which result in an alternative restructuring or insolvency process being adopted.

This chapter will address how the jurisdiction is exercised, how the exercise of that discretion may result in alternative insolvency processes being adopted and the possibility of obtaining injunctive relief.

(b) Discretion

By paragraph 13(1), on hearing an administration application the court may:

(a) "make the administration order sought;

(b) dismiss the application;

(c) adjourn the hearing conditionally or unconditionally;

(d) make an interim order;

(e) treat the application as a winding-up petition and make any order which the court could make under section 125;

(f) make any other order which the court thinks appropriate."

The discretion provided to the court by this provision is of a wide and general nature and is not constrained in any way; it should be exercised judicially, taking into account the interest of all relevant parties and the purpose of the legislation.[118]

The factors which may be relevant to the exercise of the court's discretion are multifarious and will vary on a case-by-case basis.[119] It is nevertheless possible to identify the following factors which are likely to be relevant in most cases.

(c) The views of creditors

In considering whether to exercise its discretion to make an administration order, the court's starting point will generally be to identify the wishes of the company's creditors. This is understandable as where the company is insolvent, it is the creditors who will have the predominant economic interest in the company.[120] Accordingly, where the conditions for making an administration order are satisfied, the interests of the company's shareholders will ordinarily attract comparatively little weight.[121] Similarly, the interests of secured creditors

---

[118] *Rowntree Ventures Ltd v Oak Property Partners Ltd* [2017] EWCA Civ 1944 at [24]; [2018] BCC 135.

[119] ibid.

[120] *BTI 2014 LLC v Sequana SA* [2022] UKSC 25; [2022] 3 WLR 70 per Lord Reed at [83].

[121] *Legacy Education Alliance International Limited v Progression Limited* [2019] EWHC 3498 (Ch) at [10].

weigh lighter in the scales than the interests of other creditors because they do not stand to lose so much[122].

It follows that where an administration application (whether made by the company/its directors or a creditor) is not opposed by any creditors, it is very likely that an administration order will be made[123] (although in *Re Imperial Motors UK Ltd,*[124] Hoffmann J (as he then was) refused to exercise his discretion to make an administration order on the application of a secured creditor in circumstances where the company's director personally undertook to discharge the debt of the only supporting unsecured creditor and the evidence demonstrated that if this was done, the company would be balance sheet solvent).

Conversely, where an administration application made by a company or its directors is opposed by one or more creditors and there are no supporting creditors, that will be a particularly powerful factor militating against the making of an administration order.

The position is likely to be more difficult where a creditor's administration application is opposed by other creditors or an application by the company or its directors is supported by some creditors and opposed by others; in that case, the court will need to make a value judgment as to what it is in the best interests of the company's creditors as a whole.[125]

In practice, there are two principal reasons why creditors may oppose the making of an administration order. First, they may contend that

---

[122] *Re Consumer and Industrial Press Ltd* (1988) 4 BCC 68.

[123] For example, in *Legacy Education Alliance International Limited v Progression Limited* [2019] EWHC 3498 (Ch), the court refused a debtor company's application to adjourn a creditor's administration application to enable it to prepare a CVA proposal.

[124] (1989) 5 BCC 214.

[125] See *Legacy Education Alliance International Limited v Progression Limited* [2019] EWHC 3498 (Ch) at [9].

liquidation is the more appropriate insolvency process. There are a number of reasons why this may be the case, which we will consider further below. Second (and less commonly), they may contend that a restructuring process such as a CVA or restructuring plan under Part 26A of the Companies Act 2006 is more appropriate.[126]

(d) The advantages of liquidation

In most cases where the court is considering whether to exercise its discretion to make an administration order, it will have already concluded that administration is more likely to produce a better outcome for the company's unsecured creditors than an immediate liquidation.

However, there remain a number of reasons why a creditor may contend, and the court may accept, that it is nevertheless appropriate for the company to enter into immediate liquidation.

First, as Warren J identified in *El Ajou v Dollar Land (Manhattan) Ltd*,[127] in compulsory liquidation *"the official receivers start off as liquidator, and any replacement, will be under the control of the creditors generally. There will not only be independence of office-holder from those connected with the company, but that independence will be seen to be assured."* This will be a particularly relevant consideration where the administration application has been issued by the company or its directors in response to a threatened or presented winding up petition. However, it is not necessarily determinative since in appropriate case the court could

---

[126] For example, in *NGI Systems & Solutions Ltd v The Good Box Co Labs Ltd* [2023] EWHC 274 (Ch); [2023] Bus LR 562, a company was placed into administration on its own application but the court subsequently directed the administrators to cause it to consent to a restructuring plan where it was satisfied that this would produce a better result for the creditors.

[127] [2005] EWHC 2861 (Ch); [2007] BCC 953 at [25].

appoint an alternative insolvency practitioner to act as administrator (which we will discuss in the next chapter).

Second, in a compulsory liquidation, by s.132, the official receiver has a statutory duty to investigate the company's failure and its business and dealings and affairs, and may make such report to the court as the official receiver thinks fit. In an appropriate case an investigation may provide a very important service to the creditors and a report to the court may benefit the creditors and the wider public interest.[128]

Third, on the making of an administration order, any extant winding up petition is automatically dismissed,[129] meaning that any dispositions of property made by the company after the presentation of the winding-up petition will not be rendered void by s.127 (as they would be if the company entered compulsory liquidation on the petition). Accordingly, in a case where there is evidence of significant post-petition dispositions, the court may consider it more appropriate to call on the extant petition and either appoint a provisional liquidator[130] or make a winding up order on it.[131] However, the point is likely to have little or no weight as regards unknown transactions.[132]

Fourth, sections 238 and 239 empower an office-holder to bring claims in respect of transactions at an undervalue entered into and preferences given by a company at a "relevant time". For these purposes, the relevant

---

[128] *Re Bowen Travel Limited* [2012] EWHC 3405 (Ch); [2013] BCC 18 at [39].

[129] Insolvency Act 1986, Sch.B1, para.40(1)(a).

[130] See *Re Brown Bear Foods Ltd* [2014] EWHC 1132 (Ch); *Re Officeserve Technologies Limited* [2017] EWHC 906 (Ch); [2017] BCC 363.

[131] Whilst paragraph 13(e) empowers the court to treat an administration application as a winding up petition, this would not assist because by s.129(1)(a) the subsequent winding up will be deemed to commence on the date the order is made.

[132] *Hartley Pensions Limited v Wilton UK (Group) Limited* [2023] EWHC 1700 (Ch) at [103].

period is calculated by reference to the "onset insolvency". If a winding up order is made on an extant winding up petition, this will be the time of the presentation of that petition,[133] whereas if an administration order is made on a subsequent application, this will be the date on which the application was made.[134] In that case, a winding up order would encompass more potential claims for the benefit of creditors (conversely, where there is no extant winding up petition, it would arguably be preferable for the court to make an administration order, as if the court treated the application as a winding-up petition and made a winding up order under paragraph 13(1)(e), the winding up would be deemed to commence on the making of the order[135]).

(e) Comparison of outcomes

As we discussed in the previous chapter, in order to establish that the court has jurisdiction to make an administration order, the applicant needs only to demonstrate that there is a real prospect of one of the statutory purposes of administration being achieved. In the case of objective (b), this means showing that achieving a better result for creditors is a realistic outcome; in the case of objective (c), it means showing that making a distribution to preferential or secured creditors without unnecessarily harming the interests of the unsecured creditors. Thus, the applicant does not need to show that there is no prospect of there being a worse outcome for the unsecured creditors in administration. However, the degree of risk of such outcome and the extent to which a potential outcome might be worse in administration

---

[133] Insolvency Act 1986, s.129(2) and s.240(3)(e).

[134] Insolvency Act 1986, s.240(3)(a).

[135] See *Re Gate Ventures plc* [2020] EWHC 709 (Ch) at [47].

than in liquidation are relevant factors when it comes to the exercise of the court's discretion to make an administration order.[136]

Moreover, where an administration would produce only a trivial benefit as compared to a liquidation and there are other factors which favour the liquidation, the court may conclude that it is inappropriate to make an administration order.[137]

(f) Making a winding up order

Paragraph 13(1)(e) permits the court to treat an administration application as a winding-up petition and make any order which the court could make on such a petition under section 125. This is an extremely useful power in a case where the court is satisfied that the company is irretrievably insolvent but is not satisfied that there is a real prospect of the purpose of administration being achieved or, in any event, considers that liquidation is more appropriate. However, it does not enable the court to make a winding up order where the applicant would not otherwise have standing to obtain such an order.[138]

As noted above, where there is already an extant winding up petition, the court may call it on and make an order on that petition and in most cases, this is likely to be more appropriate than making an order under paragraph 13(1)(e) given that it will result in an earlier commencement date.

---

[136] *Re Baltic House Developments Ltd* [2018] EWHC 1525 (Ch); [2018] Bus LR 1531 at [28].

[137] *El Ajou v Dollar Land (Manhattan) Ltd* [2005] EWHC 2861 (Ch); [2007] BCC 953.

[138] *Re One World Logistics Freight Limited* [2018] EWHC 264 (Ch) at [53].

(g) Adjournment

By paragraph 13(1)(c), the court has the power to adjourn the hearing of an administration application conditionally or unconditionally. However, it will rarely be appropriate to exercise this discretion in a case where the jurisdictional requirements in paragraph 11 are met, given the obvious risk to creditors if an insolvent company is not immediately placed into a formal insolvency process. One such instance is where there is an extant winding up petition and the court is able to appoint provisional liquidators to hold the ring until the adjourned hearing.[139]

(h) Interim order

By paragraph 13(1)(d), the court may make an interim order which may, in particular (a) restrict the exercise of a power of the directors or the company and (b) make provision conferring a discretion on the court or on a person qualified to act as an insolvency practitioner in relation to the company.[140]

In *SB Corporate Solutions Ltd v Prescott*,[141] the court used this power to grant a creditor's without notice application for the appointment of licensed insolvency practitioners as interim managers of a company pending the hearing of an administration application in order to preserve its business and assets.

The power was also exercised in *Re MBI Hawthorn Care Ltd*[142] to appoint interim managers of various members of a group of companies.

---

[139] Accordingly, in a case where there is evidence of significant post-petition dispositions, the court may consider it more appropriate to call on the extant petition and appoint a provisional liquidator.

[140] Insolvency Act 1986, Sch.B1, para.13(3).

[141] [2012] Bus LR D91.

[142] [2019] EWHC 2365 (Ch); [2020] BCC 1.

In contrast, in *Khawaja v The Financial Conduct Authority*,[143] the court was not prepared to make an interim administration order on the urgent application of the director of a company which the subject of an extant winding up petition presented by the Financial Conduct Authority where there was no evidence that the delay until the hearing of the winding up petition would make a material difference and the Financial Conduct Authority was given insufficient time to prepare for the hearing.

(i) Injunctive relief?

The court has jurisdiction to restrain a party from issuing an administration application or indeed from making an out-of-court appointment. Authority for that proposition is *Hitcham Homes Limited v Goldentree Financial Services PLC*.[144] In *Hitcham* the company sought to restrain a qualifying floating charge holder from doing precisely the above. Though such an application was novel, ICC Judge Prentis acknowledged the circumstances in which the court could grant such relief:

> "7. As I say, everybody is agreed that this is a novel application. Notwithstanding that, it is also the position that, in theory, the court could grant an injunction restraining the exercise of a qualifying floating charge holder's rights where it was, and I am going to use the word "plain", that it was unable to exercise those rights, either because of a defect in the charge or because of the facts which had arisen. It is also conceivable that an injunction could be granted founded on the fact that the charge holder, while a creditor with a debt owed to it, was in fact a net debtor because of counterclaims and

---

[143] [2019] EWHC 2909 (Ch).
[144] [2023] EWHC 1727(Ch).

> *so forth which the company retained against it. That at least is the broad theory."*[145]

As the court has a discretion over whether to make an administration order, an applicant must satisfy the court that there is no real prospect of the court exercising its discretion to make an administration order.[146] The court held that the floating charge was presently enforceable and that the applicant had no real prospect of success in showing that it was a creditor with a debt owing to it in excess of the debt owed to the respondent such that "*the court's discretion to refuse an administration order to an acknowledged creditor would not arise*".[147]

Whilst this decision is useful in confirming the court's jurisdiction in the above respect, parties would need to consider matters very carefully before embarking on such a course. It would need to be plain that a chargeholder's charge was not enforceable at all or presently enforceable or that a debt in excess of the sums owed to the respondent is owed to it. In the latter case, even then, it is by no means clear cut that injunctive relief would be obtained given the observations of Warren J in *Hammonds v. Pro-Fit USA Ltd*,[148] that:

> "52......In particular, in the case of a cross-claim where there can be no argument about jurisdiction, it may be that the facts indicated quite clearly that an administration order would be desirable; in such a case, there would seem to me to be no reason for requiring that a creditor – who clearly has locus standi to make an application – should be forced to defeat the cross-claim as a precondition of obtaining an order."[149]

---

[145] ibid. at [7].

[146] ibid. at [10].

[147] ibid. at [51].

[148] [2007] EWHC 1998 (Ch) [2008] 2 BCLC 159.

[149] ibid. at [52].

(j) Conclusion

In summary:

- The court has a discretion to make an administration order; the discretion is open ended and wide and should be exercised judicially, taking into account the interest of all relevant parties and the purpose of the legislation.

- Relevant factors will include: (i) the views of creditors; (ii) whether the administrator could act without causing unnecessary harm; (iii) whether administration would be worse than a liquidation; (iv) enabling a wide scope of potential claims to be brought; (v) potential void dispositions.

- The court has jurisdiction to restrain a party from making an administration application provided it can be shown that there is no real prospect of the court exercising its discretion to make an administration order.

CHAPTER SIX

DISPUTES AS TO THE APPROPRIATE APPOINTEES

(a) Introduction

It is not uncommon for the parties to be unable to agree on who the administrator(s) should be. Resolving such disputes often involve the consideration of a number of factors which range from principled concerns such as perceived partiality to practical concerns such as the sufficiency of resources. The disputes may range from inter-creditor disagreements over who the administrator(s) should be to disputes between the candidate(s) proposed by a creditor and the candidate(s) proposed by the director(s) and/or the company. Whilst the principles may differ depending on the parties to the dispute, there is some crossover in terms of the principles which apply, along with general and pervasive themes of fairness and cost efficiency which run throughout. In this chapter we will discuss the principles and practical matters to consider when faced with such a dispute.

(b) Overarching principles

The same principles which the court considers in the case of appointing a liquidator apply equally to administrations.[150]

---

[150] *Med-Gourmet Restaurants Limited v Ostuni Investments Limited* [2010] EWHC 2834 (Ch); [2013] BCC 47 at [13].

Those principles were set out in *Fielding v Seery & Anor*[151] where HHJ Maddocks said *inter alia*:

> "1. The identity of the liquidator has to be considered by reference to the purpose for which he is appointed.
>
> 2. An application in relation to the appointment of the liquidator accordingly has to be considered by reference to…whether it will be conducive to both the proper operation of the process of liquidation and to justice as between all those interested in the liquidation.
>
> 3. It follows from this that, although the majority vote of the creditors will, in the normal course, prevail, creditors holding the majority vote do not have an absolute right as to the choice of liquidator.
>
> 4. The liquidator should not be a person nor be the choice of a person who has a duty or purpose which conflicts with the duties of the liquidator.
>
> 5. More specifically, the liquidator should not be the nominee of a person:
>
>   (a) against whom the company has hostile or conflicting claims; or
>
>   (b) whose conduct in relation to the affairs of the company is under investigation."[152]

The general and pervasive theme, therefore, is one of propriety and that those who have the most 'skin in the game' should ordinarily prevail.

---

[151] [2004] BCC 315.

[152] ibid. at [33].

(c) Disputes between creditors

As regards creditor v creditor, the general principle is that the views of the majority are to be given greater weight. If all else is equal – for instance, if either candidate is suitable and there are no concerns of justice being seen to be done – then it is the view of the majority of creditors (by value) which will prevail.[153] It is easy to understand why – the majority creditors are the persons who have the most 'skin in the game' and it is their wishes therefore which should be accorded greater weight.

The majority by value approach is not an absolute rule and can be displaced by practical factors. The court has pointed out that in other cases the view(s) of the majority creditor may not prevail and there might be something to counterbalance the weight given to their views.[154] This will ordinarily be where a nominated person has already made some headway towards investigating issues which will need to be dealt with in the administration. Those circumstances would tend towards appointing that candidate to stave off the delay and cost in appointing an alternative candidate who would have to start from scratch. The same is consistent with the principle that an insolvency process should be progressed and resolved as quickly and cheaply as possible.

Hence, and as a general principle, the court will be more inclined towards a proposed appointee who has pre-existing knowledge of the company's affairs[155] – that would usually be the applicant's nominated person(s) because they will have assessed the company's position to satisfy themselves that the objectives in paragraph 3 can be met.[156] It may also be the case that the appointment of two officeholders will be perceived as

---

[153] *Healthcare Management Services Ltd v Caremark Properties Ltd* [2012] EWHC 1693 (Ch); [2013] BCC 484 at [28].

[154] ibid. at [29].

[155] *Re Maxwell Communications Corp Plc (No.1)* [1992] BCC 372.

[156] *Lightman & Moss on The Law of Administrators and Receivers of Companies* (6th ed) at 6-051.

more expensive than the appointment of one[157] – however, the counterargument may be that the work will take longer if only one administrator is appointed and could only be costs neutral at best and more expensive in the worst case.

Sometimes it is not possible to determine who the majority creditor is. In such circumstances this is simply an aspect that is eliminated from consideration, and it is the other factors which we discussed above that will usually have a part to play. In *Stanley International Betting Ltd v Stanleybet UK Investments Ltd*,[158] It was not possible to determine who in terms of value was the majority creditor between C1 (the applicant for the administration order) and C2. The court appointed C1's choice of administrator because C2 had not established to the court's satisfaction that the creditors at large could not have confidence in C1's chosen candidate to conduct a thorough and vigorous investigation to the extent necessary. In this case, there was no suggestion that sufficiency of resources or delay was a material factor such that this was a rare case where all things were truly equal and the court, in effect, adopted a presumption that the applicant's choice would be ordered unless a good reason was shown to the contrary. There is faint support for such an approach elsewhere[159] (albeit in a slightly different context) although as below this authority is not free from criticism.

Stanley has also been the subject of further criticism; the editors of *Lightman & Moss on The Law of Administrators and Receivers of Companies* 6th Ed suggest that[160] the approach in *Oracle (Northwest) Ltd v Pinnacle*

---

[157] *Institute of Chartered Accountants in England and Wales and others v Webb* [2009] EWHC 3461 (Ch); [2010] Bus LR D37 at [11].

[158] [2011] EWHC 1732 (Ch); [2011] B.C.C. 691.

[159] *Bank of Scotland Plc v Targetfollow Properties Holdings Limited* [2010] EWHC 3606 (Ch); [2013] BCC 817.

[160] *Lightman & Moss on The Law of Administrators and Receivers of Companies* (6th ed) at 6-051.

Financial Services (UK) Ltd[161] and *Re The Taylor Gallery*[162] is better because *inter alia* it is not easy to challenge a proposed candidate's probity.

We discuss the approach taken in *Oracle* below.

(d) Disputes between creditors & directors/the company

In *Med-Gourmet* the court said:

> "14. There is a public interest in office holders charged with the administration of an insolvent estate not only acting but being seen to be acting in the best interest of the creditors generally; and ensuring that all legitimate claims that the company may have are thoroughly investigated. This is a reflection of a more general principle that justice must not only be done but must be seen to be done. The importance of the principle is reflected, amongst other ways, in the fact that applications for recusal are almost always made not on the ground of actual bias but on the ground of appearance of bias."[163]

So, where creditors lack confidence in the proposed nominee's ability to conduct a thorough and vigorous investigation, the court may well appoint the nominee proposed by the creditors, this being a reflection of justice being seen to be done.[164]

In our view, a party must have reasonable grounds for lacking confidence to engage the principle that justice should be seen to be done. Whilst in practice that is unlikely to be a high bar for a party to reach, it does cull

---

[161] [2008] EWHC 1920 (Ch); [2009] BCC 159.
 [2014] NiCh 9.
[163] *Med-Gourmet Restaurants Limited v Ostuni Investments Limited* [2010] EWHC 2834 (Ch); [2013] BCC 47 at [14].
[164] ibid.

the spurious, ill-conceived and imaginary concerns that individuals may have.

In *GP Noble Trustees Ltd v Directors of Berkeley Berry Birch Plc*[165] the court acceded to a major creditor's choice over the directors' proposed nominee. It was relevant that the creditor was a very substantial one and it was therefore "*important in those circumstances that it should be seen that there is a rigorous and independent professional analysis of what is in the best interests of the creditors by whichever administrators are appointed*"[166] Whilst the directors' proposed candidate was already acting in relation to the company's subsidiary, there was no evidence before the court about the amount of the economies of scale that would arise by having the same firm of accountants involved in the administration of the whole group. Had there been, then this may well have tipped the scales in favour of the directors' candidate.

In *Oracle (Northwest) Ltd v Pinnacle Financial Services (UK) Ltd*[167] it was said that where significant creditors have a clear preference for one administrator over another, in circumstances where secured and other creditors remain neutral, the court should favour the wishes of those creditors '*for whose benefit in the end the administration is*'.[168] In that case, the issue of pre-existing familiarity with the company was not raised and the court's approach was more general, with a focus on the wishes of creditors.

However, in *Re Professional Computer Group Limited*[169] the court appointed the company's choice of administrator over the proposed

---

[165] [2006] EWHC 982 (Ch); [2007] BPIR 1271.

[166] ibid. at [12].

[167] [2008] EWHC 1920 (Ch); [2009] BCC 159.

[168] ibid. at [21].

[169] [2008] EWHC 1761 (Ch).

candidate put forward by a creditor of the company. The court did so on the footing that:

- The company's proposed candidate was familiar with the majority of the relevant matters, was experienced and qualified and there were no doubts about her integrity and *bona fides*;

- The only challenge was that the directors of the company selected their candidate and the directors needed to be investigated – however, the court was not satisfied this was a case where a party had '*gone to great lengths to install and maintain an office holder in office*';[170]

- During the course of the hearing, the creditor put forward for the first time a candidate of their own who was willing to act. However, as the court put it:

    "*58.......The real difficulty which the court has about the proposal to appoint [the creditor's nominee] Miss Thompson is that the court, unfortunately, knows next to nothing about her circumstances. The Company itself was only told of her identity during [the creditor's] submissions in court, and so the Company could not be expected to provide the court with any information one way or the other about Miss Thompson. I do not have a CV from Miss Thompson. I do not know how quickly she will be able to act. I do not know whether there will be any difficulty due to the fact that her office is in a different part of the country from where the Company's activities are principally based, whereas [the Company's nominee] Miss Fitzpatrick is nearer those activities. I do not know anything about Miss Thompson's fees. Finally, unlike Miss Fitzpatrick, Miss Thompson will need to take time to acquaint herself with all the history of the matter and with the affairs of the*

---

[170] ibid.

> *Company. In those circumstances, I do not feel that I can approve the appointment of Miss Thompson as administrator."* [171]

- Whilst the court did consider the appointment of a third person, the time involved with getting a third party up to speed in circumstances where the company did not have that time would harm the company.

- Although it did place weight on how justice must be seen to be done, the court considered that it needed to adopt a balance exercise and the arguments in favour of the creditor's approach were *"outweighed by the need to get on with this administration and by the fact that Miss Fitzpatrick is suitable in all respects apart from the suggested difficulty due to the fact she has been nominated by the directors of the Company or by the Company."*[172]

Where there are no reasons for believing that a company's or a director's nominated administrator is unlikely to be independent – in other words where there are no reasonable grounds for a lack of confidence – it is normally inappropriate to 'hold a head count' of creditors to decide between the company's/director's choice and the creditors' choice of administrator; in *Re World Class Homes Ltd*[173] the court acknowledged that a head count is unreliable and one cannot know what weight to attach to their preferences unless one knows exactly what was said to creditors. As the court put it:

> *"11…..Unless one knows really what was said to creditors, one does not know what weight to attach to their preference. If, for example, a creditor is told that the only prospect of getting a decent recovery is to have Mr A as administrator, that could have procured a support for*

---

[171] ibid. at [58].

[172] ibid. at [61].

[173] [2004] EWHC 2906 (Ch); [2005] 2 BCLC 1.

Mr A, even if it transpires that Mr B would be quite as good as Mr A. I am, therefore, not at all persuaded that there is anything conclusive in a head count of creditors."[174]

However, the court did go on to suggest that a head count could be taken into account if creditors had received/given a proper explanation as regards the choice of proposed administrators:

"12......Therefore, had it been compelling that the weight of the head count was almost wholly one way and was well explained, I think perhaps I could have taken account of it and attached some weight to it, but in the particular circumstances of this head count I am not persuaded that it pushes me to any real extent in favour of one or against another."[175]

Whilst the above decision may appear to cut against the principle that the majority view will ordinarily prevail, in practice, it will usually be sufficient for the court to know that the majority by value prefer one appointee over another; where an administration is urgently required, the court is more likely to take such an approach rather than holding a 'stewards' enquiry' to ascertain the basis behind the way in which creditors have voted. A belt and braces approach would be to summarise any information given to creditors in support or against a particular nominee.

In *Re Wolf International Ltd* [176] concerned a company which was run by a father and his son. The father was the company's director who appointed administrators via the out of court process. The son applied to cross-examine one of the joint administrators and the father, because of concerns he had about the joint administrator's independence. There was also an application by the son challenging the validity of the

---

[174] ibid. at [11].

[175] ibid. at [12].

[176] [2021] EWHC 500 (Ch).

appointment. The court refused the application to cross-examine but did not determine the validity application. However, the court granted the father's application to appoint the joint administrators (the identity of the appointees also being disputed) and such order was made with retrospective effect such that it took effect from the date of the out of court appointment.

The court suggested that the basis of an officeholder's appointment and the fact that the son was not a creditor of the company were sufficient answers to the principle of justice being seen to be done:

> *"5. As to the public interest point made by Lewison J and the need to preserve appearances, it seems to me that there are adequate safeguards in the nature of insolvency practitioners' appointments – they are officers of the court and they are heavily regulated – that adequately cover that. However, there is another factor as well, which is that Richard has no true interest here. He is not a creditor. He does not assert that he is a creditor. So, even if his father's position is not precisely that of the independent creditor contemplated by Patten J in Oracle, he is certainly a lot nearer to that state than Richard is, and to that extent it seems to me that it is likely that I am going to find that that position is going to be preferred in any event, though w have not got there yet. What I am sure about for the moment is that cross-examination is not going to assist so I refuse it."*[177]

It is certainly questionable to cite the fact that officeholders are officers of the court and are regulated as a counterpoint to justice being seen to be done – that is the starting point anyway.

In terms of the contest regarding who the administrator should be, the son sought the appointment of two new administrators or in the alternative a third party on his own or to act alongside the current administrators. The son suggested that there might be matters which

---

[177] ibid. at [5].

were liable to be reviewed by another insolvency practitioner; however the court decided:

- There was nothing in the administrators' conduct "*that has been other than the usual conduct that involves necessary contact in the run up to the administration*"[178]

- The joint administrators had helped trade the company, carried out investigations and had incurred fees such that "*the circumstances militate strongly in favour of keeping them in place*".[179]

(e) A middle ground – joint appointment?

It is perfectly possible for there to be a joint appointment where both parties proposed nominees are appointed. Whilst attractive and seemingly equitable at first blush, normally, it will be inappropriate to appoint joint IPs from different firms because it can potentially lead to an increase in time and costs.[180]

The court's views in *Oracle* supports this line of thinking:

"*20. ... I have considered the possibility of a joint appointment, because on the face of it, at least at first blush, it appeared to me to be a way out of the difficulties which I have outlined. But on further reflection I think it may create more problems than it solves. There is no evidence before me that the two sets of administrators have agreed either what the strategy of the administration should be, or how the tasks are going to be properly shared between them. In those circumstances, there is potentially the risk if a joint appointment is made of there being*

---

[178] ibid. at [13].

[179] ibid. at [13].

[180] *Re Structures & Computers Ltd*, [1998] BCC 348 at 358A.

disagreement in relation to the key issues which I have mentioned, and of there being further applications to the court for directions by the administrators, with all the costs and delays that those will entail. I certainly, as things stand today, cannot be confident that those disputes will not arise, and a joint appointment would therefore, in my judgment, simply postpone the dispute which I have to rule on this morning to a later date, and would serve, therefore, no useful purpose. I am not, therefore, prepared to make a joint appointment."[181]

It is of course possible for there to be a joint appointment if it is possible to demonstrate precisely the opposite of what the court was concerned about above. Such matters fall properly to be dealt with in witness evidence by the proposed administrator; provided it can be shown that a joint appointment would be workable and unlikely to cause additional time and cost to be incurred, the court is likely to give serious consideration to such a proposal.

The possibility of a joint appointment was considered in *Re Wolf International Ltd*[182] where the court acknowledged that had the administration been far more substantial that there might have been grounds for a joint appointment. However, the size of the administration in that case didn't warrant the additional layer of costs:

"14. Were this a much more substantial administration I might be able to see some case for appointing joint administrators, that is to say two camps of administrators, but the fact is that this is, by modern standards, a fairly small company. It is likely to be, I hope, a fairly small administration. It seems to me that the cost of an extra administrator really cannot be justified. So for those very brief reasons I will re-appoint Messrs Bass and Pagden."[183]

---

[181] [2008] EWHC 1920 (Ch); [2009] BCC 159 at [20].

[182] [2021] EWHC 500 (Ch).

[183] [2008] EWHC 1920 (Ch); [2009] BCC 159 at [14].

(f) Intervention by a QFCH?

It should be noted that a QFCH may intervene and invite the court to have their specified person appointed as administrator. In the case of an unsecured creditor versus a QFCH, the QFCH will generally be able to have its choice of administrator appointed by virtue of paragraph 36 (although the court may still appoint the unsecured creditor's nominee if it thinks it right to do so because of the particular circumstances of the case).

There have been, so far as the authors are aware, no reported cases in which this has occurred. One would think, however, that many of the principles which apply when considering a contest between rival proposed appointees will apply; accordingly, propriety and cost efficiency will likely be relevant. The views of other creditors will be less relevant because the QFCH will be a creditor and has a pre-existing right to intervene.

If it transpires that a party's charge is not a 'qualifying' floating charge (as defined in paragraph 14(2) we consider that the court may nevertheless place a great degree of weight on the floating charge holder's views, given that the administrator will be given power to deal with the charged assets as if they were not subject to security (by paragraph 70) and the costs and expenses of administration, preferential debts and the prescribed part will be payable in priority to the chargeholder's claims. This will particularly be the case where the purpose of the administration is that in para 3(1)(c). Of course, if the security is invalid (i.e it is not a floating charge at all), then the purported floating charge holder would simply be an unsecured creditor and the dispute would be resolved according to orthodox principles.

(g) Summary of principles

In essence the principles are these:

- As regards creditor(s) v creditor(s) – the majority by value will prevail unless it can be shown that it will save time and cost in using a candidate who is already familiar with the company's affairs.

- As regards creditor(s) v director(s), if creditors lack confidence in the directors' proposed nominee's ability to conduct a thorough and vigorous investigation, the court may appoint the creditor's choice in order to ensure that justice is seen to be done. Even if there are no grounds for lacking confidence, the wishes of creditors will usually prevail. Again, this may not be so when the director's candidate is already familiar with the company's affairs.

- Whilst it is inappropriate to hold a head count of creditors to decide between the company's choice and the opposing party's choice of administrator, unless one knows what has been said to the creditors, in practice, the court is unlikely to second guess the views of creditors.

- A QFCH will generally be able to have its nominee appointed under paragraph 36. As between an unsecured creditor and a mere floating charge holder, we consider that the court may place a great degree of weight on the floating chargeholder's views.

(h) Practical considerations

Depending on which side of the argument one happens to be on, it is sensible in a case where a candidate has already made headway in investigating a company's affairs to explain in detail the steps that have been taken. The more detailed the explanation, the easier it becomes to suggest that appointing a new candidate will simply increase time and cost with no countervailing benefits for the creditors.

One should also focus on the scale and resources of a proposed appointee; a company with a nationwide scale is likely to be more attractive than a smaller regional concern for the simple reason that they will have the ability and resources to progress the administration much faster.

Equally, where parties lack confidence in a proposed candidate, it is important, again, to be as detailed as possible about why that is. This helps stave off any argument that there are no reasonable grounds for lacking confidence in the proposed appointee.

CHAPTER SEVEN

PROCEDURE

The procedural aspects of an administration application are contained in rr.3.1-3.15 IR.

(a) Administrator's statement & consent to act

Rule 3.2 IR envisions that those who seek to apply for an administration order will already have consulted with the potential future administrator,[184] as an administrator's statement and consent to act will be required – an administration order is simply an order appointing a person to be an administrator of the company.

There are no prescribed forms for an administrator's statement and consent to act – the document must contain, as per r.3.2(1)(a)-(h) IR:

a) "identification details for the company immediately below the heading;

b) a certificate that the proposed administrator is qualified to act as an insolvency practitioner in relation to the company;

c) the proposed administrator's IP number;

d) the name of the relevant recognised professional body which is the source of the proposed administrator's authorisation to act in relation to the company;

---

[184] *Insolvency Litigation: A Practical Guide (3rd ed)* at 6-011.

e) a statement that the proposed administrator consents to act as administrator of the company;

f) a statement whether or not the proposed administrator has had any prior professional relationship with the company and if so a short summary of the relationship;

g) the name of the person by whom the appointment is to be made or the applicant in the case of an application to the court for an appointment; and

h) a statement that the proposed administrator is of the opinion that the purpose of administration is reasonably likely to be achieved in the particular case."

The statement and consent to act must be authenticated and dated by the proposed administrator.[185] Where a number of persons are proposed to act jointly or concurrently as administrators, each person must make a separate statement and consent to act.[186]

(b) The administration application

There is no standard form of the application itself, though a very helpful precedent may be found at the following Government Website: https://www.gov.uk/government/publications/form-comp-8-rule-33-administration-application

The application needs to comply with r.3.3 IR. Typically, the most common questions which a practitioner is faced with is whether the company is an Article 1.2 undertaking and whether the proceedings will be COMI proceedings, establishment proceedings or proceedings to

---

[185] r.3.2(2) IR.
[186] r.3.2(3) IR.

which the EU Regulation as it has effect in the law of the United Kingdom does not apply.

An Article 1.2 Undertaking, as per r.1.2 IR is:

a) "an insurance undertaking;

b) a credit institution;

c) an investment undertaking which provides services involving the holding of funds or securities for third parties;

d) a collective investment undertaking".

It is simply a question of ascertaining whether the company in question falls within any of those categories.

As to whether the proceedings will be COMI proceedings, or otherwise, a brief foray into history is required. Before the United Kingdom withdrew from the European Union, Regulation (EU) 2015/848 on insolvency proceedings (the so called 'Recast Insolvency Regulation') applied. The Recast Regulation ceased to apply from the end of the transition period on 31 December 2020. At the end of the transition period, the Recast Insolvency Regulation was retained albeit in an amended form via the Insolvency (Amendment) (EU Exit Regulations) 2019 ("**the Retained Regulations**").[187]

COMI is no more than shorthand for the "centre of main interests". The "centre of main interests" (or COMI) is *"the place where the debtor conducts the administration of its interests on a regular basis and which is*

---

[187] The Insolvency (Amendment) (EU Exit) Regulations 2019 (2019 No.146) (subsequently amended by The Insolvency (Amendment) (EU Exit) Regulations 2020 (2020 No.647)).

ascertainable by third parties".[188] For companies/legal persons, the rebuttable presumption is that the COMI is the location of the registered office.[189] In most cases, therefore, where the Company's registered office is in the United Kingdom, it will be necessary to state that these are COMI proceedings.

Establishment under the Retained Regulations has the same meaning as under the Recast Regulation, namely, any place of operations where a debtor carries out (or has carried out in the three-month period prior to the request to open insolvency proceedings) a "non-transitory economic activity with human means and assets".[190] This will be, for instance where, a company's COMI is located elsewhere, but there are separate business premises in the United Kingdom.

As for circumstances where the Retained Regulations will not apply, this will be where there is no registered office,[191] or where, in the United Kingdom, the Company does not have its COMI or an establishment, and the company sought to be placed into administration is one which is either, by paragraph 111;[192]

(a) "a company registered under the Companies Act 2006 in England and Wales or Scotland;

(b) a company incorporated in an EEA State..., or

---

[188] Regulation (EU) 2015/848 of The European Parliament and of The Council of 20 May 2015, Article 3(1).

[189] ibid.

[190] ibid, Article 2(10).

[191] r.1.7 IR.

[192] See *Re Nektan (Gibraltar) Ltd* [2020] EWHC 65 (Ch); [2020] B.C.C 331 on the interaction between paragraph 111 and the court's jurisdiction to place a company into administration.

(c) a company not incorporated in an EEA State but having its centre of main interests in a member State (other than Denmark [....]."

(c) Supporting witness statement

The witness statement in support must comply with r.3.6 IR and must therefore contain:

(a) "a statement of the company's financial position, specifying (to the best of the applicant's knowledge and belief) the company's assets and liabilities, including contingent and prospective liabilities;

(b) details of any security known or believed to be held by creditors of the company, and whether in any case the security is such as to confer power on the holder to appoint an administrative receiver or to appoint an administrator under paragraph 14 of Schedule B1;

(c) a statement that an administrative receiver has been appointed if that is the case;

(d) details of any insolvency proceedings in relation to the company, including any petition that has been presented for the winding up of the company so far as known to the applicant;

(e) where it is intended to appoint a number of persons as administrators, a statement of the matters relating to the exercise of their functions set out in paragraph 100(2) of Schedule B1;

(f) the reasons for the statement that the proceedings will be COMI proceedings, establishment proceedings or proceedings to which the EU Regulation as it has effect in the law of the United Kingdom does not apply; and

(g) any other matters which, in the applicant's opinion, will assist the court in deciding whether to make such an order."

In practical terms this will mean, for the purposes of paragraph (a) above, that an application made by directors (or, indeed, the company itself) should provide:

- the latest Internal financial reports and projections accompanied with an explanation of when the company will become insolvent;[193]

- evidence of unfulfilled demands for payment (if applicable);

- information regarding the company's banking and finance arrangements and whether any such arrangements are in jeopardy or have been exhausted.[194]

For the purposes of paragraph (d) above, a search should be undertaken of the central register for whether a winding up petition has been presented,[195] or indeed by carrying out a search via the Gazette.

---

[193] *Insolvency Litigation: A Practical Guide* (3rd ed) at 6-019.
[194] ibid.
[195] ibid.

(d) What should be filed with the court?

As per r.3.7 IR, the application, supporting witness statement and the administrators consent to act should be filed at court, together with a certificate of service, below. Sufficient copies of the application should be filed for the purposes of service.

(e) Service of the application

A sealed copy of the application and witness statement in support should be served.[196] The proposed administrator's statement and consent to act should be appended to the witness statement in support.[197]

The following should be served, pursuant to r.3.8(3)(za)-(f)

- "any person who has appointed an administrative receiver of the company;

- any person who is or may be entitled to appoint an administrative receiver of the company;

- any person who is or may be entitled to appoint an administrator of the company under paragraph 14;

- If there is a moratorium in force for the company under Part A1 of the Act, the monitor;

- any administrative receiver of the company;

---

[196] r.3.8 IR.

[197] *Insolvency Litigation: A Practical Guide* (3rd ed) at 6-018.

- if there is a petition pending for the winding up of the company on—(i) the petitioner, and (ii) any provisional liquidator;

- the company, if the application is made by anyone other than the company or its directors;

- any supervisor of a CVA in relation to the company;

- the proposed administrator.

- any enforcement agent or other officer who to the knowledge of the applicant is charged with distress or other legal process against the company or its property

- any person who to the knowledge of the applicant has distrained against the company or its property

- The Regulator, if the company is, or has been, an authorised person or recognised investment exchange, is, or has been, an appointed representative; or is carrying on, or has carried on, a regulated activity in contravention of the general prohibition.[198] The FCA and the PRA are entitled to be heard at the hearing of an administration application and the applicant will also need to serve the documentation upon them.[199]

(f) How may service be effected?

Service of an administration application is to be carried out in accordance with paragraph 3 of Schedule 4 IR by delivering the documents as follows:

---

[198] Financial Services and Markets Act 2000, s.362(1).

[199] *Insolvency Litigation: A Practical Guide* (3rd ed) at 6-012.

- on a company at its registered office or if service at its registered office is not practicable at its last known principal place of business in England and Wales; and

- on any other person at that person's "proper address" (i.e. any address which he has previously notified as the address for service, but if the person has not notified such an address then the documents may be served at that person's usual or last known address).

If it is impracticable to effect service as provided for above, then by virtue of paragraph 1(5) Schedule 4 IR, service may be effected in such other manner as the court may approve or direct.

For service outside of the jurisdiction, this must be in accordance with CPR Part 6[200] and in addition, when service is to be effected in an EU Member State, the Hague Convention of 15 November 1965 on the service abroad of judicial and extrajudicial documents in civil and commercial matters.

In any case, the applicant is required to file with the court a certificate of service which must be filed with the court as soon as reasonably practicable after service and in any event not later than the business day before the hearing of the application.[201]

(g) QFCH intervention?

If a QFCH seeks under paragraph 36(1)(b) to have a specified person appointed as administrator, the holder must produce to the court—

---

[200] Para.1(8), Sch,4 IR.

[201] r.3.8(4) IR.

- the written consent of the holder of any prior qualifying floating charge

- the proposed administrator's consent to act; and

- sufficient evidence to satisfy the court that the holder is entitled to appoint an administrator under paragraph 14 of Schedule B1.[202]

(h) Application by a QFCH?

An application by a QFCH who does not wish to exercise the powers under their security document via the out of court procedure should follow the procedure in paragraph 35(1), the contents of which are self-explanatory.

(i) Determining the application

The court will fix a venue for the hearing of the application. An administration application may be dealt with by a High Court Judge or ICC Judge (but not a District Judge Sitting in a District Registry or a District Judge).[203] Where the application is issued in London, it will be listed in the ICC Judge's Applications List.[204] Accordingly, the applicant's advocate will be required to sign and file a certificate of urgency.[205]

---

[202] r.3.11(1) IR.

[203] PDIP, para.3.3.(1).

[204] Chancery Guide, para.21.48(a).

[205] Chancery Guide, para.21.49.

The following persons may appear and be represented at the hearing of the application:[206]

- "the applicant;

- the company;

- one or more of the directors;

- if there is a moratorium in force for the company under Part A1 of the Act, the monitor;

- any administrative receiver;

- any person who has presented a petition for the winding up of the company;

- the proposed administrator;

- the holder of any qualifying floating charge;

- any supervisor of a CVA;

- with the permission of the court, any other person who appears to have an interest which justifies appearance."

The court will then follow the steps and consider the matters we have already covered as part of its determination of whether or not to make an administration order.

---

[206] r.3.12(1) IR.

CHAPTER EIGHT

RETROSPECTIVE ADMINISTRATION ORDERS

(a) Introduction

Errors in the process of placing a company into administration via the out of court route which were incapable of being characterised as mere formal defects or irregularities gave rise to the recognition and (at times uncomfortable) adoption by the courts of the retrospective administration order. There are several cases[207] which deal with such matters, and it may be that the jurisdiction of the court to grant a retrospective administration order results in a contested administration application (including arguments as the existence of the court's jurisdiction to make such an order). In this chapter, we shall focus on that jurisdiction and its interaction with a contested administration application.

---

[207] *Minmar (929) Ltd v Khalastchi* [2011] EWHC 1159 (Ch); [2011] BCC 485; Hill v Stokes plc [2010] EWHC 3726 (Ch); [2011] BCC 473; *Re Assured Logistics Solutions Ltd* [2011] EWHC 3029 (Ch); [2012] BCC 541; *Westminster Bank plc v Msada Group Ltd* [2011] EWHC 3423 (Ch); [2012] BCC 485; *Re Virtualpurple Professional Services Ltd* [2011] EWHC 3487 (Ch); *Re Ceart Risk Services Ltd* [2012] EWHC 1178 (Ch); [2012] BCC 541; *Re BXL Services Ltd* [2012] EWHC 1877 (Ch); [2012] BCC 657; *Re Euromaster Ltd* [2012] EWHC 2356 (Ch); [2013] Bus LR 466; *Re G-Tech Construction Ltd* [2007] BPIR 1275; *Re Kaupthing Capital Partners II Master LP Inc* [2010] EWHC 836 (Ch); [2011] BCC 338; *Re M.T.B Motors Ltd* [2010] EWHC 3751 (Ch); [2012] BCC 601; *Re Frontsouth (Witham) Ltd* [2011] EWHC 1668 (Ch); [2011] BCC 635.

(b) Jurisdiction & the test

Whilst it has been questioned, it is (for now at least) settled that the court has jurisdiction to grant an administration order that will have retrospective effect.[208] The pragmatic appeal of such a course is that making that order validates[209] actions taken by purported administrators during a time period where the validity of their appointment lay in doubt. It should be noted that a retrospective appointment can take effect no more than 364 days before the order is made, *"because the period of office would have expired by the time of the making of the order and there would be no ability to extend the term of office from its expiry under the (retrospective) court order."*[210] It is of course open to the court to grant a retrospective order followed immediately by an extension of the same pursuant to paragraph 76.

There have been numerous cases which considered the validity of a purported administration appointment where the appointor: (i) failed to give prior notice of their intention to appoint the administrator to one or

---

[208] *Gregory v A.R.G. (Mansfield) Ltd* [2020] EWHC 1133 (Ch); [2020] BCC 641 at [122]. However, in *Re Synergi Partners Ltd* [2015] EWHC 964 (Ch); [2015] BCC 333 at [12]-[19] and *Re Elgin Legal Ltd* [2016] EWHC 2523 (Ch); [2017] BCC 43 at [17]-[18], HHJ Hodge QC and Snowden J (as he then was) identified a number of powerful arguments against the existence of the power to make an appointment with retrospective effect and the issue has not yet been considered at appellate level.

[209] It should be noted in this context that validation simply means that those actions will be treated as actions carried out as administrators as opposed to trespassers. It does not amount to approval of those actions in the sense of whether they were correct or not, *Re ARL O09 Ltd* [2020] EWHC 3350 (Ch) at [65]-[68].

[210] *Re Mederco (Cardiff) Ltd* (09477164) [2021] EWHC 386 (Ch); [2021] BCC 597 at [28]

more of the persons specified in the Act or the Rules; and/or (ii) filed a notice of appointment in the wrong prescribed form.[211]

It should be noted that there are seemingly infinite ways an administration appointment can go wrong and the above are examples only. It is possible for instance that an administrator's (validly appointed) term of office expires due to a failure to follow the procedure correctly in paragraph 76(2)(b).[212]

When errors come to light anxious consideration is subsequently given to whether the appointment of the administrators is valid – a matter of significant import because if not, the purported administrators are effectively trespassers[213] which can have serious ramifications for such individuals if they have dealt with and disposed of company assets. Accordingly, and depending on the type and degree of the error which causes the legitimacy of their purported appointment to be in doubt, the purported administrators may be able to seek a declaration that they have been validly appointed and will where circumstances allow rely upon r.12.64 IR (which provides that no insolvency proceedings will be invalidated by any formal defect or any irregularity unless the court before which objection is made considers that substantial injustice has

---

[211] *Minmar (929) Ltd v Khalastchi* [2011] EWHC 1159 (Ch); [2011] BCC 485; *Hill v Stokes plc* [2010] EWHC 3726 (Ch); [2011] BCC 473; *Re Assured Logistics Solutions Ltd* [2011] EWHC 3029 (Ch); [2012] BCC 541; *Westminster Bank plc v Msada Group Ltd* [2011] EWHC 3423 (Ch); [2012] BCC 485; *Re Virtualpurple Professional Services Ltd* [2011] EWHC 3487 (Ch); *Re Ceart Risk Services Ltd* [2012] EWHC 1178 (Ch); [2012] BCC 541; *Re BXL Services Ltd* [2012] EWHC 1877 (Ch); [2012] BCC 657; *Re Euromaster Ltd* [2012] EWHC 2356 (Ch); [2013] Bus LR 466 ; *Re G-Tech Construction Ltd* [2007] BPIR 1275; *Re Kaupthing Capital Partners II Master LP Inc* [2010] EWHC 836 (Ch); [2011] BCC 338; *Re M.T.B Motors Ltd* [2010] EWHC 3751 (Ch); [2012] BCC 601; *Re Frontsouth (Witham) Ltd* [2011] EWHC 1668 (Ch); [2011] BCC 635.

[212] *Re Mederco (Cardiff) Ltd* (09477164) [2021] EWHC 386 (Ch); [2021] BCC 597.

[213] *Re ARL 009 Ltd* [2020] EWHC 3350 (Ch) at [64].

been caused by the defect or irregularity and that the injustice cannot be remedied by any order of the court) to support that declaration. However, where that relief is not available, it will be necessary to seek a fresh administration order with retrospective effect.

The juridical basis which justifies the court in being able to make a retrospective administration order is contained in paragraph 13(2) which provides:

> "(2) An appointment of an administrator by administration order takes effect—
>
> (a) at a time appointed by the order, or
>
> (b) where no time is appointed by the order, when the order is made."

As the court held in *Re Skeggs Beef Ltd*,[214] cases concerning defective out-of-court administration appointments can be divided into three categories:

> (1) 'Cases where the defect is fundamental' – in those circumstances the purported administration appoint is a nullity, the further consequence being that no insolvency proceedings were ever started such that there is nothing on foot for the court to cure.
>
> (2) 'Cases where the defect is not fundamental and causes no substantial injustice'. In these cases, the court if satisfied that the defect or irregularity has caused no "substantial injustice" will make the declaration required by r.12.64 IR.
>
> (3) 'Cases where the defect is not fundamental, but substantial injustice is caused'. In such cases, the court must ask itself whether that injustice can be remedied via a court order. If it can

---

[214] [2019] EWHC 2607 (Ch); [2020] BCC 43.

be, the court will assess whether it should go on to make a remedial order to cure the position, thereby rendering the appointment valid. If the court cannot make a remedial order or does not wish to make one then the defect remains uncured. In such circumstances, it is suggested that the defect will render the appointment invalid, as per the wording of r.12.64.

The question when a rule or provision has been broken is ultimately whether the breach results in there being a procedural defect or whether in fact the breach means that the appointment is a nullity that can be dealt with only by the making of a retrospective administration order. That measure is not, properly understood, a cure at all; it is simply a party starting from scratch in placing a company into administration. Thus, courts are of course alive to the difference between a procedural defect and one which is more fundamental in nature.[215]

The court has endorsed what has been referred to as the *Soneji*[216] approach. That is, when determining the effect of a breach of statute or rules, the court should consider, in light of the consequences of non-compliance, whether as a matter of statutory construction, it was intended by Parliament that an appointment made in breach of the relevant provision would be a nullity.[217]

In that regard, there is a difference between provisions which define the scope of circumstances in which a power to appoint arises and those which prescribe procedural requirements which must be fulfilled before an appointment is properly made. Failure to comply with the former will amount to a nullity, whereas non-compliance with the latter would result

---

[215] *Gregory v A.R.G. (Mansfield) Ltd* [2020] EWHC 1133 (Ch); [2020] BCC 641 at [91].

[216] *R v Soneji* [2005] UKHL 49; [2006] 1 AC 340.

[217] *Gregory v A.R.G. (Mansfield) Ltd* [2020] EWHC 1133 (Ch); [2020] BCC 641 at [44].

in the appointment being irregular, but valid.[218] In practical terms, this would mean that r.12.64 IR could potentially regularise the position.

By way of example, an appointment of administrators out of court by an inquorate board of directors would be a fundamental defect that concerned the power to appoint – the purported appointment would be defective and could not be rectified via r.12.64 IR.[219] Conversely, the failure to give a QFCH the requisite 5 business days' notice of intention to appoint an administrator is a procedural requirement that should be fulfilled before an appointment is properly made, however it produces an irregularity which can be cured.[220]

The court has resolved disputes as to whether a breach results in the appointment being a nullity or instead an appointment which suffers from a technical defect by asking the following questions:

(1) "What are the statutory requirements regarding the appointment?

(2) If the statutory requirements have been breached, is the consequence, as a matter of construction of the provisions, that there is only a procedural defect or is the appointment a nullity?

(3) If the appointment is subject to a procedural defect, is substantial injustice caused by what would otherwise be validation under r12.64?

(4) If there is such substantial injustice, can this be remedied by Court order?

---

[218] *Re Euromaster Limited* [2012] EWHC 2356 (Ch); [2012] BCC 7 at [27].
[219] *Re Minmar (929) Ltd* [2011] EWHC 1159 (Ch); [2011] BCC 485.
[220] *Strategic Advantage SPC v Rutter* [2020] EWHC 3171 (Ch).

(5) If the appointment is a nullity, can and should the defect be cured by a retrospective order?" [221]

However, in some cases,[222] the court has avoided the need to resolve such disputes altogether by adopting the pragmatic approach first taken by Mann J in *Re Bradford Bulls (Northern) Ltd*[223] of making a retrospective administration order, together with an order under paragraph 79 providing that if and insofar as the administrators were already validly appointed, that appointment shall come to an end on the date from which the retrospective administration order takes effect.

There is a growing willingness by courts to uphold the validity of appointments;[224] that willingness being entirely proper as in most cases it cannot sensibly have been intended that a breach of requirements would result in an appointment being a nullity. The existence of technical defects in many cases will not produce any substantial injustice and should not detract from the bigger picture which is that there needs to be an administration. It is also consistent with the more general principle that form ought to not generally prevail over substance.

---

[221] *Gregory v A.R.G. (Mansfield) Ltd* [2020] EWHC 1133 (Ch); [2020] BCC 641 at [91].

[222] *Re London Oil and Gas Ltd* [2020] EWHC 35 (Ch); *Gregory v A.R.G. (Mansfield) Ltd* [2020] EWHC 1133 (Ch); [2020] BCC 641, *Re Mederco (Cardiff) Ltd* [2021] EWHC 386 (Ch); [2021] BCC 597.

[223] [2016] EWHC 3557 (Ch); [2017] BCC 50.

[224] *Strategic Advantage SPC v Rutter* [2020] EWHC 3171 (Ch); *Re Skeggs Beef Ltd* [2019] EWHC 2607 (Ch); [2020] BCC 43; *Hill v Stokes plc* [2010] EWHC 3726 (Ch); [2011] BCC 473; *In re Virtualpurple Professional Services Ltd* [2011] EWHC 3487 (Ch), [2012] BCC 254.

(c) In context

As with any other administration application, an application for a retrospective administration order can only be made by one of the prescribed persons in paragraph 12.

In the case of an administrator who was at one stage validly appointed but whose term of office inadvertently expired, such an individual will have standing as a creditor to apply for the administration order if they had fees due to them which relate to the period where they were validly appointed.[225]

If the administrators were never validly appointed then the authors suggest that they are still creditors in the sense that they will have carried out work for the benefit of the company, and on the mutual understanding that they would be paid for the same (after all, we are concerned with a defective appointment rather than a principled rejection to there being an administrator at all). The difficulty is that a court would very possibly be unattracted to allowing a party who was never validly appointed to rely on work which they had never carried out in their capacity as an administrator of the company to obtain standing status.

What is more likely (and eminently the safer and more sensible option) is that the directors or indeed the company itself will make the application (although this may not necessarily be practically achievable). If the defect is considered fundamental (or there is any doubt in this regard), they will seek the appointment of the same administrator albeit with retrospective effect to the date that they were initially purportedly appointed.

---

[225] *Re Elgin Legal Ltd* [2016] EWHC 2523 (Ch); [2017] BCC 43 at [24], *Re Mederco (Cardiff) Ltd* (09477164) [2021] EWHC 386 (Ch); [2021] BCC 597 at [47].

It is at that juncture that a challenge may be mounted against such a course. For example, a creditor may have harboured doubts and disappointment over the manner in which the administration was progressing, the propriety of the purported administrator or indeed may have felt that the company should have been placed into liquidation from the very outset. That creditor may therefore wish for the company to be placed into liquidation instead or indeed may accede to the administrator being appointed with retrospective effect but then immediately seek their removal and replacement with a candidate of their own choice, see paragraph 91.

In *Re London Oil and Gas Ltd*[226], a QFCH applied for a retrospective administration order on the basis that an out-of-court appointment may have been invalid. The director of the company objected both to the (re)appointment of the purported administrators and to the making of the order with retrospective effect (and reserved the right to argue that there is no jurisdiction to make such order should the matter reach the Court of Appeal). Whilst ICC Judge Jones was prepared to make a fresh appointment of the purported administrators, he declined to deal with the application for the appointment to have retrospective effect (which was adjourned generally with liberty to restore).[227]

It is important to recognise that whether or not the statutory criteria for making an administration order are made out is to be determined both at the date of the application and the earlier date from which it is to have effect. Accordingly, it is not sufficient that those requirements would have been satisfied at the date of the purported appointment if they are

---

[226] [2020] EWHC 35 (Ch).

[227] ibid. See also *Re Wolf International Limited* [2021] EWHC 500 (Ch), in which the director's son objected to the making of a retrospective administration order and sought the appointment of alternative administrators.

no longer satisfied by the time of the hearing.[228] The significance of that, is that it is theoretically possible that by the time of the administration application, matters have progressed to the extent that none of the objectives in paragraph 3 can be achieved such that there are no grounds for making an administration order. Admittedly, the circumstances would need to be unusual for that to have happened.

Whether an administration should take place or instead a liquidation will also fall to be resolved by orthodox principles which we have already covered as part of the court's discretion on whether or not to make an administration order. Here the court's task may be easier; it will likely be furnished with real material that demonstrates how the 'administration' was progressing – if it is overwhelmingly clear that it would be in the best interests of creditors overall for the status quo, as it were, to continue, then that would be the likely outcome. The opposite we venture to think is also true.

We think that save for an extreme case where there are real doubts about the propriety of the former purported administrator, or where the 'administration' has only just begun (and even then it would be questionable) the court is very unlikely to appoint a new administrator. The time and cost consequences will likely have a deleterious effect on other creditors.[229]

---

[228] *Re Care Matters Partnership Ltd* [2011] EWHC 2543 (Ch) at [11]; [2011] BCC 957.

[229] See *Re London Oil and Gas Ltd* [2020] EWHC 35 (Ch) at [40] and *Re Wolf International Limited* [2021] EWHC 500 (Ch) at [13].

CHAPTER NINE

COSTS

(a) Introduction

As always, this is a matter of significant import. The key issues concern the costs of the unsuccessful party who opposed the application and the potential liability of directors for making such an application. We discuss the same below.

(b) Unsuccessful party?

If the court makes an administration order, the costs of the applicant and any other person appearing whose costs are allowed by the court are payable as an expense of the administration, by r.3.12(2) IR. No costs statement is required – it is usually better for an officeholder to assess one's costs as opposed to the court, as the latter will usually be less generous.[230]

But what about the costs of a party who has unsuccessfully opposed the making of the administration order?

In *Re Structures & Computers Ltd*[231] the court allowed the costs of a majority creditor who opposed a company's application for an

---

[230] By r.12.42(1) IR, where the costs of any person are payable as an administration expense, the amount payable must be decided by detailed assessment unless agreed between the administrator and the person entitled to payment. However, in practice, it is extremely rare for an office-holder to require a detailed assessment to take place.

[231] [1998] BCC 348.

97

administration order. The costs judgment is remarkably brief and is worthy of repeating in full:

> *"To order that a party opposing the making of an administration order should receive his costs as part of the administration when the court had thought it right to make an administration order is unusual. Nonetheless, this is an unusual case and I do not think it would be just to make any other order. As I indicated during argument, the arguments and points made on behalf of [the opposing creditor] not merely caused me considerable doubts as to whether to make an administration order but, perhaps more importantly on this issue, have caused me to make certain observations about the conduct of the administration which will find their way into the order the court makes.*
>
> *I think on the exceptional facts of this case and bearing in mind that, anyway, [the opposing creditor] is having to bear the majority of the shortfall anyway as a major creditor of the company, it is the right order to make in this case. It reflects the justice of the case and that is the order I make."*[232]

This approach was doubted in *Re Professional Computer Group Limited*[233] where a creditor who unsuccessfully opposed an administration order was also refused its costs to be an expense of the administration. The court's rationale was that:

- If the creditor had not objected, the court would have made an administration order and the costs of the company would have been less than they actually were.

- The creditor ultimately failed in its opposition, something out of the ordinary would be required to justify an order for an

---

[232] [1998] BCC 348 at 358G-H.

[233] [2008] EWHC 1541 (Ch); [2009] BCC 323.

unsuccessful party's costs to be paid as an expense. The court questioned the suggestion in *Structures* that a party who places doubt in the court's mind as to whether or not to make an administration order was a sufficient reason for that party to obtain its costs as an expense.

- The creditor was not the only creditor, and making a costs order in their favour would impact other creditors.

- Guidance was given on the position of the unsuccessful creditor:

> *"30.....In my judgment, a creditor who does oppose an administration application should reason as follows. If its opposition succeeds then it has secured the benefit which it wished to secure. It will also in a typical case obtain an order for costs against the company applying for the administration order. If its opposition fails then the creditor should not expect that it will automatically obtain an order for its costs as an expense of the administration. However, an unsuccessful creditor may be able to persuade the court that the facts of the particular case are exceptional and that it is in all the circumstances just that its costs of its opposition to the order should be paid as an expense of the administration. In my judgment, that state of affairs is unlikely to deter a creditor from putting forward reasonable arguments in opposition to an administration application. I will deal separately, later in this judgment, with the cases in which the court might make an order for costs against an unsuccessful opposing creditor".*[234]

Accordingly, the test has become considerably more stringent; the circumstances would need to be exceptional (perhaps because of conduct issues) and it would need to be in all the circumstances just that such an order for costs is made. It seems clear that merely advancing good (but

---

[234] ibid. at [30].

ultimately failed) opposition to the making of an administration order will be insufficient by itself to tip the scales.

The court also went on to make an order that part of the company's costs would be paid by the creditor. The court did so on the following bases:

- On the question of principle: the court held it would only make an order for costs against the creditor where it considered it just in all the circumstances to so order. The court recognised that even where a creditor's submissions were not successful, they may well have made a worthwhile contribution. If the court could order a creditor's costs to be an expense, it followed that it could in an appropriate case make an order that the creditor pay the company's costs.

- The company's costs were increased by the creditor's opposition, the burden of which impacted the company and the creditors and because the company's assets were modest, may have been significant.

- The creditor's submissions were rejected on jurisdiction, discretion and on the appropriate appointee.

- The principle that costs followed the event was an effective way of doing justice between the parties and that overall, the creditor had not given any sufficient reason which meant that it was just for the company to pay its own costs.

In *Re Wolf International Ltd*,[235] the facts of which we have discussed above, the son, very late in the day conceded that the company needed to enter administration and indeed lost almost every point he had taken.

---

[235] [2021] EWHC 500 (Ch).

The court in no uncertain terms did not think it proper to award his costs against any party:

> "22. The second point, it seems to me, is this: there is absolutely no question of Richard being awarded any costs against anyone, notwithstanding Mr Fennell's gallant attempts to put up a case for him having some. The fact is that he has hindered rather than helped. He has concentrated on minute issues that are much more to do with the feud between himself and his father, than they are to do with the good of the company. It is, I suspect, for that reason that he has ultimately conceded, but only ultimately and very late in the day, the need for the company to go into administration. As to that, as indeed generally, he has lost on almost every point he has taken. I say that, bearing in mind, of course, that some have not been decided."[236]

As he had raised issues which had not been pursued/raised issues which he had lost, it was right that a costs order be made against the son. In respect of the administration application, the court held that the son pay 25% of the costs of the same. The son was also ordered to pay 65% of the administrators' costs of the application which sought to challenge the validity of the out of court appointment along with 60% of the father costs in respect of the same.

Such cases may appear alarming to parties who seek to oppose an administration order. However, it would be unusual for the court to make such an order; the authors are unaware of any other cases in which such an order has been made. It is certainly easier to see, given the court's comments *in Re Wolf International Ltd*[237] why a cost order was made in that case. In practice, the court is unlikely to make such an order save for extreme circumstances. It should also be borne in mind that the increase in the company's costs in *Re Professional Computer Group Limited*[238] was

---

[236] ibid. at [22].

[237] ibid.

[238] [2008] EWHC 1541 (Ch); [2009] BCC 323.

alleged to be significant and in others that may not be the case. The key takeaway is a need to ensure that grounds of opposition are properly formulated and rigorously assessed in terms of their merits; the better the grounds of opposition, the less likely it seems to us that a court would have sympathy with an applicant's request that a creditor pay part of the company's costs.

(c) Directors' liability?

Directors are potentially liable for the costs of an administration application. In *Re W.F. Fearman Ltd (No. 2)*[239] an application for an administration order made by directors was subsequently withdrawn and the court made a winding up order. The court ordered that the directors should bear the costs which they had incurred in respect of the administration application, notwithstanding that (what is now) r.3.4 IR provides that after an administration application made by directors is filed, it is treated as an application by the company itself. The court's rationale was that even though the directors had acted bona fide, that, in and of itself, did not justify the prejudice which would be caused to creditors by allowing those costs to rank as an expense in the winding up.

The potential harshness of this principle was softened in *Re Gosscourt (Groundworks) Ltd.*[240] In that case, the company applied for an administration order some five days after the presentation of a winding up petition. On the first hearing of the administration application, the company did not seek to support the administration application which was subsequently dismissed. A winding up order was then made without any opposition from the company. The court allowed the company's costs of the administration application to the date of the first hearing to be paid as an expense in the winding up and refused to make a costs order against one of the directors personally. This was because it was satisfied

---

[239] (1988) BCC 141.
[240] (1988) BCC 372.

that the administration application had been presented in good faith, reasonably and on the advice of an insolvency practitioner.

That the acid test was whether the application has been made reasonably was shown in *Re Land and Property Trust Co plc*.[241] In that case, the court ordered the directors of a company who applied for an administration order to pay an opposing party's costs on a joint and several basis. Key to this finding *inter alia* was that:

- there was no evidence that the directors had received any advice on whether an administration was suitable by the time they resolved to make an application for an administration order; and

- the application was persisted with in the face of overwhelming opposition and was not abandoned, in circumstances where the court concluded it was extremely unlikely that the statutory purpose of the administration would be achieved.

The test was made somewhat more stringent in *Re Tajik Air Ltd*.[242] The court held that the test for whether a director should be ordered to pay the costs of a failed administration application is whether reason and justice require the directors to pay the costs. Reason and justice will not usually require a director to pay costs unless they have caused costs to be incurred for an improper purpose, for instance, if a director sought to obtain a private advantage at the expense of creditors or to conceal their wrongdoings.

Accordingly, the position is that directors will not ordinarily be liable to pay the costs of a failed administration application. It will need to be demonstrated that the directors had caused costs to be incurred for an improper purpose.

---

[241] [1991] BCC 446.
[242] [1996] BCC 368.

MORE BOOKS BY
LAW BRIEF PUBLISHING

A selection of our other titles available now:-

'A Practical Guide to the Independent School Standards – September 2023 Edition' by Sarah McKimm
'A Practical Guide to Estate Administration and Crypto Assets' by Richard Marshall
'A Practical Guide to Managing GDPR Data Subject Access Requests – Second Edition' by Patrick O'Kane
'A Practical Guide to Parental Alienation in Private and Public Law Children Cases' by Sam King QC & Frankie Shama
'Contested Heritage – Removing Art from Land and Historic Buildings' by Richard Harwood QC, Catherine Dobson, David Sawtell
'The Limits of Separate Legal Personality: When Those Running a Company Can Be Held Personally Liable for Losses Caused to Third Parties Outside of the Company' by Dr Mike Wilkinson
'A Practical Guide to Transgender Law' by Robin Moira White & Nicola Newbegin
'A Practical Guide to 'Stranded Spouses' in Family Law' by Mani Singh Basi
'A Practical Guide to Residential Freehold Conveyancing' by Lorraine Richardson
'A Practical Guide to Pensions on Divorce for Lawyers' by Bryan Scant
'A Practical Guide to Challenging Sham Marriage Allegations in Immigration Law' by Priya Solanki
'A Practical Guide to Digital Communications Evidence in Criminal Law' by Sam Willis
'A Practical Guide to Legal Rights in Scotland' by Sarah-Jane Macdonald
'A Practical Guide to New Build Conveyancing' by Paul Sams & Rebecca East
'A Practical Guide to Defending Barristers in Disciplinary Cases' by Marc Beaumont
'A Practical Guide to Inherited Wealth on Divorce' by Hayley Trim
'A Practical Guide to Practice Direction 12J and Domestic Abuse in Private Law Children Proceedings' by Rebecca Cross & Malvika Jaganmohan

'A Practical Guide to Confiscation and Restraint' by Narita Bahra QC, John Carl Townsend, David Winch
'A Practical Guide to the Law of Forests in Scotland' by Philip Buchan
'A Practical Guide to Health and Medical Cases in Immigration Law' by Rebecca Chapman & Miranda Butler
'A Practical Guide to Bad Character Evidence for Criminal Practitioners by Aparna Rao
'A Practical Guide to Extradition Law post-Brexit' by Myles Grandison et al
'A Practical Guide to Hoarding and Mental Health for Housing Lawyers' by Rachel Coyle
'A Practical Guide to Psychiatric Claims in Personal Injury – 2nd Edition' by Liam Ryan
'Stephens on Contractual Indemnities' by Richard Stephens
'A Practical Guide to the EU Succession Regulation' by Richard Frimston
'A Practical Guide to Solicitor and Client Costs – 2nd Edition' by Robin Dunne
'Constructive Dismissal – Practice Pointers and Principles' by Benjimin Burgher
'A Practical Guide to Religion and Belief Discrimination Claims in the Workplace' by Kashif Ali
'A Practical Guide to the Law of Medical Treatment Decisions' by Ben Troke
'Fundamental Dishonesty and QOCS in Personal Injury Proceedings: Law and Practice' by Jake Rowley
'A Practical Guide to the Law in Relation to School Exclusions' by Charlotte Hadfield & Alice de Coverley
'A Practical Guide to Divorce for the Silver Separators' by Karin Walker
'The Right to be Forgotten – The Law and Practical Issues' by Melissa Stock
'A Practical Guide to Planning Law and Rights of Way in National Parks, the Broads and AONBs' by James Maurici QC, James Neill et al
'A Practical Guide to Election Law' by Tom Tabori
'A Practical Guide to the Law in Relation to Surrogacy' by Andrew Powell
'A Practical Guide to Claims Arising from Fatal Accidents – 2nd Edition' by James Patience
'A Practical Guide to the Ownership of Employee Inventions – From Entitlement to Compensation' by James Tumbridge & Ashley Roughton
'A Practical Guide to Asbestos Claims' by Jonathan Owen & Gareth McAloon

'A Practical Guide to Stamp Duty Land Tax in England and Northern Ireland' by Suzanne O'Hara
'A Practical Guide to the Law of Farming Partnerships' by Philip Whitcomb
'Covid-19, Homeworking and the Law – The Essential Guide to Employment and GDPR Issues' by Forbes Solicitors
'Covid-19 and Criminal Law – The Essential Guide' by Ramya Nagesh
'Covid-19 and Family Law in England and Wales – The Essential Guide' by Safda Mahmood
'A Practical Guide to the Law of Unlawful Eviction and Harassment – 2nd Edition' by Stephanie Lovegrove
'Covid-19, Brexit and the Law of Commercial Leases – The Essential Guide' by Mark Shelton
'A Practical Guide to Costs in Personal Injury Claims – 2nd Edition' by Matthew Hoe
'A Practical Guide to the General Data Protection Regulation (GDPR) – 2nd Edition' by Keith Markham
'Ellis on Credit Hire – Sixth Edition' by Aidan Ellis & Tim Kevan
'A Practical Guide to Working with Litigants in Person and McKenzie Friends in Family Cases' by Stuart Barlow
'Protecting Unregistered Brands: A Practical Guide to the Law of Passing Off' by Lorna Brazell
'A Practical Guide to Secondary Liability and Joint Enterprise Post-Jogee' by Joanne Cecil & James Mehigan
'A Practical Guide to the Pre-Action RTA Claims Protocol for Personal Injury Lawyers' by Antonia Ford
'A Practical Guide to Neighbour Disputes and the Law' by Alexander Walsh
'A Practical Guide to Forfeiture of Leases' by Mark Shelton
'A Practical Guide to Coercive Control for Legal Practitioners and Victims' by Rachel Horman
'A Practical Guide to the Law of Driverless Cars – Second Edition' by Alex Glassbrook, Emma Northey & Scarlett Milligan
'A Practical Guide to TOLATA Claims' by Greg Williams
'A Practical Guide to Elderly Law – 2nd Edition' by Justin Patten
'A Practical Guide to Responding to Housing Disrepair and Unfitness Claims' by Iain Wightwick

'A Practical Guide to the Law of Bullying and Harassment in the Workplace' by Philip Hyland
'How to Be a Freelance Solicitor: A Practical Guide to the SRA-Regulated Freelance Solicitor Model' by Paul Bennett
'A Practical Guide to Prison Injury Claims' by Malcolm Johnson
'A Practical Guide to the Small Claims Track – 2nd Edition' by Dominic Bright
'A Practical Guide to Advising Clients at the Police Station' by Colin Stephen McKeown-Beaumont
'A Practical Guide to Antisocial Behaviour Injunctions' by Iain Wightwick
'Practical Mediation: A Guide for Mediators, Advocates, Advisers, Lawyers, and Students in Civil, Commercial, Business, Property, Workplace, and Employment Cases' by Jonathan Dingle with John Sephton
'The Mini-Pupillage Workbook' by David Boyle
'A Practical Guide to Crofting Law' by Brian Inkster
'A Practical Guide to the Law of Domain Names and Cybersquatting' by Andrew Clemson
'A Practical Guide to the Law of Gender Pay Gap Reporting' by Harini Iyengar
'NHS Whistleblowing and the Law' by Joseph England
'Employment Law and the Gig Economy' by Nigel Mackay & Annie Powell
'A Practical Guide to Noise Induced Hearing Loss (NIHL) Claims' by Andrew Mckie, Ian Skeate, Gareth McAloon
'An Introduction to Beauty Negligence Claims – A Practical Guide for the Personal Injury Practitioner' by Greg Almond
'Intercompany Agreements for Transfer Pricing Compliance' by Paul Sutton
'Zen and the Art of Mediation' by Martin Plowman
'A Practical Guide to the SRA Principles, Individual and Law Firm Codes of Conduct 2019 – What Every Law Firm Needs to Know' by Paul Bennett
'A Practical Guide to Adoption for Family Lawyers' by Graham Pegg
'A Practical Guide to Industrial Disease Claims' by Andrew Mckie & Ian Skeate
'A Practical Guide to Conducting a Sheriff Court Proof' by Andrew Stevenson
'A Practical Guide to Vicarious Liability' by Mariel Irvine
'A Practical Guide to Applications for Landlord's Consent and Variation of Leases' by Mark Shelton
'A Practical Guide to Relief from Sanctions Post-Mitchell and Denton' by Peter Causton

'A Practical Guide to Equity Release for Advisors' by Paul Sams
'A Practical Guide to Financial Services Claims' by Chris Hegarty
'The Law of Houses in Multiple Occupation: A Practical Guide to HMO Proceedings' by Julian Hunt
'Occupiers, Highways and Defective Premises Claims: A Practical Guide Post-Jackson – 2nd Edition' by Andrew Mckie
'A Practical Guide to Financial Ombudsman Service Claims' by Adam Temple & Robert Scrivenor
'A Practical Guide to Running Housing Disrepair and Cavity Wall Claims: 2nd Edition' by Andrew Mckie & Ian Skeate
'A Practical Guide to Holiday Sickness Claims – 2nd Edition' by Andrew Mckie & Ian Skeate
'Arguments and Tactics for Personal Injury and Clinical Negligence Claims' by Dorian Williams
'A Practical Guide to Drone Law' by Rufus Ballaster, Andrew Firman, Eleanor Clot
'A Practical Guide to Compliance for Personal Injury Firms Working With Claims Management Companies' by Paul Bennett
'RTA Allegations of Fraud in a Post-Jackson Era: The Handbook – 2nd Edition' by Andrew Mckie
'RTA Personal Injury Claims: A Practical Guide Post-Jackson' by Andrew Mckie
'On Experts: CPR35 for Lawyers and Experts' by David Boyle
'An Introduction to Personal Injury Law' by David Boyle

These books and more are available to order online direct from the publisher at www.lawbriefpublishing.com, where you can also read free sample chapters. For any queries, contact us on 0844 587 2383 or mail@lawbriefpublishing.com.

Our books are also usually in stock at www.amazon.co.uk with free next day delivery for Prime members, and at good legal bookshops such as Wildy & Sons.

We are regularly launching new books in our series of practical day-to-day practitioners' guides. Visit our website and join our free newsletter to be kept informed and to receive special offers, free chapters, etc.

You can also follow us on Twitter at www.twitter.com/lawbriefpub.

Simon Passfield KC is a leading insolvency barrister who heads the insolvency team at Guildhall Chambers. He was called to the Bar in 2009 and was appointed as a King's Counsel in 2024. Simon has appeared in over 50 reported insolvency cases, including a number of leading cases concerning contested administration applications (*Re Officeserve Technologies Ltd* [2017] EWHC 906 (Ch); *Re Baltic House Developments Ltd* [2018] EWHC 1525 (Ch)), applications to restrain the appointment of administrators (*Hitcham Homes Ltd v Goldentree Financial Services plc* [2023] EWHC 1727 (Ch)) and the validity of out-of-court administration appointments (*Re Bradford Bulls (Northern) Ltd* [2016] EWHC 3557 (Ch); *Re Skeggs Beef Ltd* [2019] EWHC 2607 (Ch)). Prior to taking silk, he was a member of the Attorney General's Regional A Panel of Junior Counsel to the Crown. He has sat as a Deputy Insolvency and Companies Court Judge since 2020.

Govinder Chambay is a specialist insolvency practitioner who practises from Guildhall Chambers. He was called to the Bar in 2018 and regularly appears in both the County Court and the High Court. He is developing a substantial insolvency practice which includes: (i) applications to extend an administration; (ii) applications to bring an administration to an end; (iii) advising on misfeasance/directors duties claims; (iv) petition/statutory demand work; (v) possession and sale applications and a wide range of other Insolvency Act applications.